Russell Simmons

# def
# POETRY
# JAM
## on
# BROADWAY
## ...and more

Russell Simmons

# def POETRY JAM on BROADWAY ... and more

## The Choice Collection

edited by **Danny Simmons, assisted by M. Raven Rowe**

conceived by **Stan Lathan and Russell Simmons**

**ATRIA** BOOKS

New York   London   Toronto   Sydney

**ATRIA** BOOKS

1230 Avenue of the Americas
New York, NY 10020

Copyright © 2003 by Russell Simmons and Stan Lathan

"Uncle Sam's Table" copyright © 2003 by Staceyann Chin

"My Jamaica" copyright © 2003 by Staceyann Chin

"My Grandmother's Tongue" copyright © 2003 by Staceyann Chin

"Blue" copyright © 2003 by Steve Colman

"Our Heroes" copyright © 2003 by Steve Colman

"Room and Bored" copyright © 2003 by Steve Colman

"tongue tactics" copyright © 2003 by Mayda Del Valle

"Seduce Me" copyright © 2003 by Mayda Del Valle

"academia leaves my tongue heavy" copyright © 2003 by Mayda Del Valle

"The Gift of Memory" copyright © 2003 by Suheir Hammad

"Nothin' to Waste" copyright © 2003 by Suheir Hammad

"The Givers" copyright © 2003 by Suheir Hammad

"The Words" copyright © 2003 by Black Ice

"The Short End of the Stick" copyright © 2003 by Black Ice

"Untitled #29384" copyright © 2003 by Black Ice

"Lemon's Haikus" copyright © 2003 by Lemon

"Aaliyah" copyright © 2003 by Lemon

"We Are Such Stuff That Dreams Are Made Of" copyright © 2003 by Georgia Me

"And You Wonder" copyright © 2003 by Georgia Me

"End of Story" copyright © 2003 by Poetri

"Urges" copyright © 2003 by Poetri

"Poet Rock Star" copyright © 2003 by Poetri

"if I was your best friend" copyright © 2003 by beau sia

"unicorn dream" copyright © 2003 by beau sia

"choices" copyright © 2003 by beau sia

"Tendaji's Top Ten Hip-Hop Joints / R&B Club Joints" copyright © 2003 by Tendaji

"I Sing of Shine" copyright © 1986 by Etheridge Knight

Design by Vertigo Design, NYC   www.vertigodesignnyc.com

Photography by Carol Rosegg

All rights reserved, including the right to reproduce this book or portions thereof in any form whatsoever. For information address Atria Books, 1230 Avenue of the Americas, New York, NY 10020

ISBN: 0-7434-7621-2
        0-7434-7622-0 (Pbk)

First Atria Books trade paperback edition March 2005

10 9 8 7 6 5 4 3 2 1

**ATRIA** BOOKS is a trademark of Simon & Schuster, Inc.

Manufactured in the United States of America

For information regarding special discounts for bulk purchases, please contact Simon & Schuster Special Sales at 1-800-456-6798 or business@simonandschuster.com

today, like yesterday,
spoken word is giving
        a voice to the voiceless

**Danny Simmons**

## PART ONE

conceived by **Stan Lathan and Russell Simmons**

written and performed by **Black Ice, Staceyann Chin, Steve Colman, Mayda Del Valle, Georgia Me, Suheir Hammad, Lemon, Poetri, Beau Sia, and DJ Tendaji**

directed by **Stan Lathan**

# ENTS

## PART TWO

# FORE\

by **Russell Simmons**

Hip-hop culture continues to evolve multidimensionally reflecting the truth of the oneness of humanity expressed in a splendid array of diversity. Poetry is the highest artistic form of hip-hop. The poet speaks from his or her heart. This love, when expressed through spoken word, should always be welcomed and cherished.

When my brother, Danny Simmons, first recommended that I join him in an attempt to take spoken word mainstream, calling it *Def Poetry Jam,* I had no idea where it would lead. Now we have a Peabody Award–winning HBO series and we enjoyed a great run on Broadway that ended with a Tony Award. My partner, Stan Lathan, used his brilliance and entertainment industry expertise to produce and direct these critically acclaimed shows. Based on an overwhelmingly positive response, we intend to share *Def Poetry* with the rest of the world.

The resurgence of poetry throughout America and around the world is a positive testimony to the irrepressible creativity of the emerging generation of youth who will not be silenced. This book is a primer on the one hand that documents the lyrical genius of the world-class poets who performed in the cast of *Def Poetry Jam on Broadway,* and on the other hand demonstrates the relevance and power of the poetic word in the twenty-first century.

The penetrating and pulsating poetry of Black Ice, Steve Colman, Poetri, Lemon, Beau Sia, Suheir Hammad, Mayda Del Valle, Staceyann Chin, Georgia Me, and DJ Tendaji present a universal message of empowerment. The

# WORD

tremendous thumbs-up response from the Broadway community was another significant fact. The mainstream, it appeared, was finally increasing its awareness and reception to the dramatic power of hip-hop poetry.

The publication of *Def Poetry Jam on Broadway* is an important milestone. Of the numerous published books on poetry, this book is unique because it fully captures the energy, emotion, and impact of the spoken word as it relates simultaneously to the contemporary theater and the hard realities of the street. It is our hope that millions of people will be further inspired to write and recite poetry.

Spitting the truth is the dynamic of hip-hop poetry that keeps it real. We are all thankful to God that *Def Poetry Jam on Broadway* is one of the books that will help open more doors and opportunities for the poets of the future.

# EDITOR

by **Danny Simmons**

*Def Poetry Jam* began as the desire of Bruce George, a spoken-word poet, to give the art form a higher profile. He dreamed of a spoken-word movement that would become a major force on the cultural landscape of America. He and his partner Deborah Pointer asked me to be the architect to make the dream a reality. The success of my brother Russell's HBO show, *Def Comedy Jam,* inspired me to call the project *Def Poetry Jam.* After some convincing, Russell consented to the use of the Def Jam brand. Nearly two years of hard work went toward building a national presence for the project—launching a website, and staging readings across the country—before the concept was mature enough for Russell and his producing partner, renowned director Stan Lathan, to become actively involved.

Stan's contribution to the *Def Poetry* project has been incalculable. He provided passion and expertise in developing, directing, and producing both the HBO and the Broadway shows. From the moment Stan emerged from an early showcase at the Brooklyn Museum, he has lived and breathed *Def Poetry.* Stan, Deborah, and I took a group of poets to the Aspen Comedy Festival and convinced HBO executives of the significance and appeal of spoken word. We succeeded and ultimately the rave responses to the television show carried us into a second and third season, which lead to the program receiving a 2003 Peabody Award.

Spoken word has flowed into mainstream American culture in a big way, and Tony Award–winning *Def Poetry Jam on Broadway* is the ultimate evidence of that. Nine racially diverse poets and a DJ were a hit on the Great White Way,

def poetry jam on broadway

spitting poems that a short time ago could only be heard in coffee shops. Our concept of taking spoken word mainstream has exceeded the expectations of even Bruce, Deborah, and myself.  Stan and Russell have helped make performance poetry, once viewed as an esoteric art form, palatable to the hearts and minds of America and beyond.  The hip-hop community has enthusiastically embraced spoken word.  City kids from all over America are joining poetry clubs and writing their thoughts in verse.  It's a good thing.  Dialogue is being promoted, and it's now hip for people to talk about what's going on inside and around them.  When I was first asked why I was promoting poetry, I told a writer, "Spoken word could probably be the most potent tool for social change America has ever seen."  Like in the 1970s when poets such as Ntozake Shange, the Last Poets, Nikki Giovanni, Sonia Sanchez, Amiri Baraka and many others were at the center of that decade's cultural movement.  Poetry again is changing how we see ourselves.  Today, like yesterday, spoken word is giving a voice to the voiceless.

# THE PR

by **Stan Lathan**

We began the process in the spring of 2002 by choosing nine poets from the dozens who had participated in the HBO series. I tried to pick the best writers and performers from varied backgrounds, so as to reflect a cross section of young artists who were influenced by hip-hop. The show had been booked for one-nighters in several cities and a short run in San Francisco. Broadway was a goal that seemed like a distant fantasy.

When the nine poets and DJ first walked into Chelsea Studios in Manhattan, I had no idea what was going to come out of the initial workshop experience. I hoped that the mixture of each poet's individual voice and style would result in a show that would make the audience reflect, laugh, learn, and be entertained. The challenge was to get this group of solo performers to become an ensemble and to have their individual poems evolve into an exciting theatrical event.

The poets brought their work to the table. They performed for one another, and they shared constructive criticism and suggestions. We also collaborated on group pieces, trios, and duets. We added musical transitions to the process. The poets worked with the DJ, blending their favorite songs with his musical choices.

After the weeklong workshop we took our loosely formed show on the road, to Phoenix, Long Beach CA, and San Diego. We experimented with different poems and orders of performance. By the time we arrived at Theatre on the Square in San Francisco, the original collaborative poems were fine-tuned, the music was pretty much in place, and the show had taken on a form that I felt was suitable for a night at the theater.

# OCESS

We formatted the show into thematic segments: introduction of poets, group poems, personal concerns, love poems, and poems of rage or protest, leading up to the exciting finale "I Write America." Stage manager Alice Smith and assistant director Mark Swinton made valuable contributions to the development of the poets into professional theater artists. I worked with set designer Bruce Ryan and lighting designer Yael Lubetsky to come up with an environment as inspired as the work of the ensemble.

We conducted an aggressive ad and marketing campaign to convince lovers of poetry, lovers of hip-hop, and lovers of theater to come share this experience with us. When the show opened in San Francisco to rave reviews and overwhelming audience response, it became obvious to Russell and me that it was time to seriously set our sights on Broadway.

With the exception of a few lines in various poems to keep up with changing times and current events, *Russell Simmons Def Poetry Jam On Broadway* turned out to be much the same as the show we worked so hard to perfect for the stage in San Francisco. For me the experience is a highlight of my long career as a director and producer of television, film, and live entertainment. Every time I see the show I am thrilled and inspired. I have learned so much about creativity and commitment from nine spoken-word artists and a DJ. And I believe that these poets and their words will influence and inspire for generations to come.

# def POETRY JAM on BROADWAY

conceived by **Stan Lathan** and **Russell Simmons**

written and performed by **Black Ice, Staceyann Chin, Steve Colman, Mayda Del Valle, Georgia Me, Suheir Hammad, Lemon, Poetri, Beau Sia,** and **DJ Tendaji**

directed by **Stan Lathan**

# act one

## PRELUDE

*written by* **The Company**

(Lights come up on the DJ. The MC begins to set the tone of the piece musically. Tendaji, the DJ introduces the poets.)

**tendaji**  New York!

**poetri**  I wanna write a poem letting everybody know
God is my light.

**mayda**  I wanna hear an Elvis is dead but Tito Puente
is still alive poem

**georgia me**  I wanna live the poem of a dirty southern bell
who through the love of God overcomes ignorance
to live free and very well.

**suheir**  I wanna be read, loved, memorized,
I wanna be a poem that changes lives

**staceyann**  I wanna hear "dat" poem about a Jamaican
Rasta man who has never smoked weed.

**black ice**  I wanna raise my poems like kids
Keep them from jail bids,
Pessimism and negativity.

**beau sia**  I want all poems to be about me

**lemon**  Let's get piss ass drunk so I can
signify a "Toast" poem

def poetry jam on broadway

# i wanna HEAR A POEM

*written by* **Steve Colman**

**steve**   I wanna hear a poem
I wanna learn something I didn't know
I wanna say 'YES' at the end
Because I'm sick of saying 'so?'

I wanna hear a poem about who you are
and what you think
and why you slam
not a poem about my poem
because I know who I am
I wanna hear a love poem a sad poem an I hate my dad poem
a dream poem an I'm not what I seem poem
an I need poem an I also bleed poem
an I'm alone poem an I can't find my home poem
I just wanna hear poem
I wanna hear a poem about revolution
about fists raised high
and hips twisting in a rumble
like a rumba
I wanna follow the footsteps of Che
and hear the truth about the day
the CIA killed Lumumba
And because every second matters
I wanna hear long poems and short poems
about time and its limits
because it took less than three minutes
to attack Abner Louima
to frame Assata Shakur

and destroy Hiroshima
to kill Eleanor Bumpers
and Anthony Baez
to gun down Malcolm with bullets they bought
from the Feds

I wanna hear a poem
where ideas kiss similes so deeply
metaphors get jealous
where the subject matters so much
that adjectives start holding pro-noun rallies
at city hall
because I want to hear a poem

that attacks the status quo
that attracts the claps of the cats
with the phattest flows
that makes the crowd
pass the hat
and pack my cap
with a stack of dough
I want to hear a poem that makes this audience
Yell HOOOOO!!!!!
Because I want to guess your favorite color
then craft rhyme schemes out of thin air
I wanna hear a poem about why the statute of
limitations
for rape
is only five years
I wanna hear a poem
I wanna feel a poem
I wanna taste a poem
Give me your spot on the mic
if you wanna waste a poem
I wanna hear a poem.

# THE county of
# KINGS

*written by* **Lemon**

**lemon**   Where I'm from...
Where I'm from is known as the boro of royalty,
the infinite party rocker
the home of the big poppa
89 door knockers,
a place where I can stick my middle finger up
in the air for that little punk ass john rocker
see I'm from the county of king where everyday we
know we fortunate to see another morning
we take our nieces and our nephews
and put 'em under our wings
send them out in that world hoping they keep
that grass green,
the county of kings
hometown to the best fighters whoever stepped
in the ring
we are still the land of the angriest
blacks puertoricans baggiest phat farmers
craziest baby mommas fire escapes,
bootleg c.ds and mixed tapes
we will always have the worst crooked cops
we will always have the most
motherfucking weed spots
The county of kings
new skool like bloods and crips
but we ole skool like the savage skulls
and chingelings
the crazy girls and black pearls

def poetry jam on broadway

shit we go way back like he-man
underwears tight bvds
pin striped lees, bums called peabody
'cuz if you ever go to the county of kings
ya ass better pass by flatbush and pick me up
a vegetable patty with cocoa bread and an
order of crown fried chicken wings
tip the eight year old boy outside the store
harlem shaking it up cause that's the way
he makes his living
see the county of kings its not the house
it's the home where I rest so when I yell out
for Brooklyn new york city
I want to hear always hear funky fresh......

# FULL FIGURE
# potential:
# A FAT GIRLS
# BLUES

*written by* **Georgia Me**

**georgia me**  Out of money looking for a snack
Then I see little Debbie's face on a pack
Smiling enticing me inviting me to have a taste
With haste I race to the destruction of my waist
As the sugar sets in so does the disgust I
feel
Wishing I had the power of will or hoping someone
Would kill this gluttonous
Monster which rules my eyes
Which is bigger than my stomach so we fill
my belly
with pies and cakes
by-products additives and other shit
It's hard for me to quit sweets are a quick hit
My diet includes fried everything all kinds of pork
People asking if I've been visited by the stork
See it's looked at as a sin to be fat without children
or a medical condition
So it leaves a girl fishing
Looking for an excuse to stop
the abuse
I endure everyday in every way through ridicule and
personal shame
Unwanted attention and fame from the group of young
men who holler "Big Drawers"

as I pass by I start to cry the wind dries my eye
But nothing can heal this scar left on my esteem
Praying this ordeal is a dream or better yet
a nightmare
For it's too hard to bare this constant scare as
my reality. A complete
disregard for humanity
Not seen as humane more like insane or having no
self control
She can't even pass up a jelly roll
Not seen as beautiful. Look at the folds and gut the
cellulite thighs and out of shape butt
Not seen as strong "She can't go long. She'll be
down before the end of the song"
My personal demons are hard by themselves
Comparisons to pigs, elephants, and whales
You might look at me and see lazy and weak giving
no second thought that
before you an angel may speak
God said
Love who you are be the best that you can be
Your spirit will soar and the whole world will see
Your strength your beauty and your heart
The ignorance of others won't pierce like a dart
I know at times I may get knocked down or even
doubt my ability
But I'll look in the mirror and say I'm wonderful
With humility
Now we're supposed to respect everyone with
Different choices beliefs and hues
But who gives a damn about a fat girls blues.

# SOMETIMES I PRETEND I'M MICHAEL JACKSON

*written by* **Poetri**

**poetri**  Sometimes
I call on my mind and make believe I'm Michael
Jackson
Suddenly I'm in the lime light since nine,
I take his life and make it mine.
Not all the time,
but every now and then,
I like to fake like I have all his friends,
the real ones and the fake ones.
I impersonate all his dance steps
the old and the latest ones.
And if you glance for a quick second, you might even
Think that I were him!
I mean, you know, if the lights were dim.
If I lost a little weight and you were standing
a couple miles away,
you could say that I favor him a little bit,
dance like him a little,
sing like him.
Sometimes I pretend I am him.
I know he's done some things that are
strange to us…
I mean why don't you try being a star
since you were a kid like I did, huh?

Why don't you try selling a gazillion records like
I did!
Boy you can't tell me nothing when I play like
Michael Jackson!
Sometimes I'm "Thriller" with an attitude
I'll tell you to "Beat it" in a minute
'cause I ain't got time to "Rock with you."

I got all the money.
I like to pretend that I can walk into a bank
and no one is following me.
I'm Michael Jackson,
I ain't gonna steal nothing!
I like to act like couples don't grab each other
when I walk by.
I like to fake like the police actually wave to me
when I drive by
I like to pretend that I am respected in every city,
    state and country.
I represent boundaries
I wish every one thought like me.
I can bring the world together sometimes
When I assume I'm Michael Jackson
Most times I portray Mike when I'm in the car
lip-synching like I'm the star.
People always look at me strange when they see me
Singing "Billie Jean" at a stop light
They must not recognize me.
So, I just keep harmonizing my troubles away
until they drive away
moonwalking through pain, prejudice and poverty,
see life right now is real hard for me

so pardon me Mr. Jackson
if I use your personality for relaxin',
I'm not crazy or nothin'.
I'm just looking for something to free my mind.
And if you don't mind, I pretend I'm you.
I pretend that I can change people through my music.
I act like people feel special when I'm around
them.
I am you...
Sometimes when I'm tired of being me.

# ...and THESE ARE only some of THE THINGS I Believe

*written by* **Staceyann Chin**

**staceyann**   Imagination is the bridge between
the things we know for sure
and the things we need to believe
When our world become unbearable

But in this world of school boy bullets,
biological warfare and kiddie porn—
it takes guts to believe in any God
so I practice on believing in the smaller things
till I am able to make room for the rest

I begin with believing there is a Santa Claus
Except I believe St. Nicolas is a holiday
transvestite
And I believe in monsters lurking under the bed
because they give our children something
to conquer, before the world begins to
conquer them

And contrary to popular belief
I believe Bert and Ernie are straight
I believe they're just waiting for the
right girls to come along
I believe bongs are pieces of art
I believe it's wrong to fart in an elevator

Then get off at the next floor
I believe whore is a word we created for women
Who liked fucking more than men.

I believe most lovers will lie to you eventually
And though I believe two wrongs don't ever make
a right— Sometimes slashing his tires makes you feel
    better

I believe Pinkie and the brain are revolutionaries
Because every night, they try to take over the
world
Like them I believe there will always be something
to fight for
So I believe in the sounds my lover makes
during sex
I believe in eating East Indian mangoes and lesbians
    from Montego Bay
I believe in believing everyday –
in fists and friendships
and final words
I believe birds were once people in
another life
I believe our lives are often shorter
Then we expect
So for as long as we can, I believe
we should believe in some things
we don't know for sure
Acknowledge the range
of possibilities not limited by what we see
move reality with imagination
we decide what our destinies will be.

# TOTALLY
# XXXTREME

*written by* **Beau Sia**

**beau**  give me a scrabble board
and watch
as I beat you
without using consonants

give me a song
any song
and I will kick your ass
at musical chairs

give me ten teenage cheerleader sluts
and my solo pyramid
will still score higher than theirs in competition

I'm that extreme sports mothafuckah
your mama warned you about

in a world of no fear, just do it,
now who's the craziest sports slogan maniacs
I'm the mentally buff Chinese hulk Hogan
disciplined, determined
and deadly
to punk ass bustas
that want to step to me

I woke up at dusk just to mock your mom
for giving birth to you

how extreme is that?

I'll go extreme on a toaster and not shed a
single tear

cuz     I ride extreme ponies.
          I take extreme bubble baths
          I even have an extreme diary.

here's an excerpt from memory

dear diary.  dusk.  woke up.

mocked the mothers of my enemies
for giving birth to them
stole a pro athlete's wheaties
shat in shaq's shoes
put Spanish fly in tiger woods' powerade
and made him cry
went to mcdonald's, had a snack at mcdonalds's
caused a scene at mcdonald's
got kicked out of mcdonald's
went home, decided to crank call the U.N.

hello?
Is this the un?
yeah uh-huh
this is beau sia
yeah      you've got a bomb!
in your pussy!

I'm senior dream team extreme.
pushing the limits

five time roman candle fight champion

intercontinental smashing little kids'
science projects champ 1999

I'm so extreme
next year's x games will be called
"beau sia makes your mangina cry"
games.

I'm so extreme
the prison system, depends diapers, and crack
are my sponsors.

I'm so extreme
I took the words "let's get ready to rumble!"
and made 'em cut it down
to just "rumble!"

# EXOTIC

*written by* **Suheir Hammad**

**suheir**  Don't wanna be your exotic
Like some delicate fragile colorful
bird imprisoned caged in a
land foreign to the stretch of her wings

Don't wanna be your exotic
Women everywhere look just
like me some taller darker
nicer than me but like me
Just the same women everywhere
carry my nose on their faces
my name on their spirits

Don't seduce yourself with my
otherness
the beat of my lashes
against each other ain't some
dark desert beat it's just
a blink get over it.

Don't build around me
your fetish fantasy your
lustful profanity to
cage me in clip my wings

Don't wanna be your exotic
your loving of my beauty ain't
more than funky fornication
plain pink perversion in
fact nasty necrophilia

because my beauty is dead
to you


Not your harem girl
geisha doll banana picker
pom pom girl   poom poom short
coffee maker town whore
belly dancer private dancer
la malinche venus hottentot
laundry girl your immaculate
vessel emasculating princess
don't wanna be
not your erotic not your exotic

# 410 days in THE LIFE

*written by* **Black Ice**

**black ice**

When you look at my brothas
What's ya' first impression?
Does the sight of us
Leave you guessin',
or do you understand the stressing?
The aggression
The look of no hope
On me and my niggas faces
like
the Lord over-looked us
when
He handed down his graces
You see...
Embraces,
fall short on the
numb tips of
street entrepreneurial fingers.
Still,
stuck in the walls
of the project halls
where
the coke smell still
lingers.
External blingers
is all we can be
because on the inside
we've been given nothing
to shine on...
and a record deal is

harder to get than coke
so,
My Niggas get their grind on.
Because , the t.v. tells us
"Aim high nigga!!"
Make all goals lateral."
But that takes paper
we don't have
so niggas put their souls
up as collateral
Now,
some niggas reclaim 'em.
Some blame 'em,
making an excuse to sell 'em.
But,
when a nigga goes from not doing,
to doing...
What can you tell 'em?
Not to be a nigga?!
I
gotta be a nigga
that's how I pay the bills.
and I'll do that
if I have to sling coke
or exploit these rhyme skills.
See,
America makes you an opportunist
and at the same time,
they institutionalize you.
So,
the fact that niggas get
big record deals,
big money,

and
then go to jail
shouldn't surprise you.
That's what lies do.
See the secret lies in these
Midtown Manhattan
Skyscrapers
Where former hustlers
Like myself sign papers
and pull off fucked up capers like
sixteen infamous stars at a time.
They got us choppin', baggin', and servin' that shit
to niggas sixteen bars at a time.
now
the crime is undetectable by the FEDS
'cause in heads of our kids
is where the track is
and music is potent
it's straight to the soul
so,
it's much more addictive
than crack is...
Now, the high is just an illusion
all lies and confusion
but to feel that rush just once...
my young bucks will go through it.
So in essence,
they're still flooding the streets
with the thugs, drugs, and killing...
They're just usin' these record labels
to do it.
Takin' our heartfelt demos
Putting us in limos

tryin' to fuck up divine direction
but
young black men have been trained
to chase money and
pussy
so we fall
victim to our own erection
and begin to convince ourselves
we're on our way
somewhere
where we're not goin'...
But,
Ignorance is bliss
and
niggas love this
so niggas take pride
in not knowing...
WE'RE NOT GROWING!!!
Nigga I give a fuck how
slick you flowin'
if you ain't showin' nothin'
to these kids
or
adding nothing positive
to the Earth...
Black Ice been destined
to touch the world ever since
I was born,
to be real,
fuck a record deal...
God
Gives me what I'm worth.

# in the COCINA

*written by* **Mayda Del Valle**

**mayda**  mami's making mambo
mami's making mambo

in the domain of the del Valle kitchen
my mother is the dictator
I refer to it as
"Carmen's culinary queendom"
She— is a cuisine conquistadora
wielding a freshly sharpened knife
like a sword above her head
here Goya doesn't stand a chance
no pre-packaged shit
she is the menu mercenary
the soldier of soul food
back the fuck up!
coz mami's making mambo
she hangs the hats of iron chefs
off the windowsill like
roast duck trophies
and laughs at the sight of any edible
food item.

Mua-ha-ha-ha-ha-ha-ha

no meat in the freezer
poof'
Spam and corned beef in a can are
transformed into virtual filet mignon

rice cooks itself instantly at her command
and beans jump into bubbling pots shrieking
Carmen please…Carmen please
cook me master please
honor me with your spice
Emeril and Julia Childs mere hamburger
flippers in her presence
It was there in my mother's kitchen that
I learned more
than how to cook
It is where
I learned the essence of rhythm and power
I learned how to dance
In the midst of clanging clave pots
and wooden mortars and pestles
she would say to me
the way to a man's heart is through his stomach
and your hips
so you better learn how to cook mija
she gave me the secret recipe for ritmo

Two and a half cups of caderas , a pound of girating
    pelvis,
a pinch of pursed lips
a tablespoon of shaking shoulders
and a generous helping of soooooouuuuuuul
combine and mix
now I,m dancing the way my mother cooks.

slow, sultry, spicy, sabrosa natural instinctively
drippin' sweet sweat like fresh leche do coco
spinnin' as fast as piraguas melt in summertime
southside heat

dancing with as much kick as cuchifrito and bacardi
standing strong like a morning time bustelo
steamy as pasteles at Christmas
blendin' my hip hop and mambo like a pina-colada
my mouth watering for music with sabor en caderas
soothes down my hips
dulce as Celia's Azzzucaaaar!
Con dulcura
I'm cooking with sabor
I'm bailando con sabor
coz
mami's making mambo
mami's making mambo
Mamucha, come eat , the food's ready.

# METAPHORS

*written by* **Steve Colman** *and* **Poetri**

| | |
|---|---|
| **steve and poetri** | Sometimes we don't understand poets |
| **steve** | They can't have normal conversations |
| **poetri** | Without slipping into flowery language<br>Or turning everything into a metaphor |
| **steve** | Yes, it can be a most laborious undertaking to disentangle oneself from a web of words willfully unwieldy, woven willy nilly word sometimes its just wack |
| **poetri** | The fact is too often a poet's imagination is overactive |
| **steve** | A thunderstorm is not divine aquatic intervention |
| **poetri** | Fall is not the season of winter's apprehension |
| **steve** | (Hey, that's kind of nice) |
| **poetri** | (Thanks...)<br>We admit that some wordsmiths aren't<br>so bad when shove comes to push |
| **steve** | But a lot of poets are like awkward cunnilingus<br>They tend to beat around the bush |
| **poetri** | And these verbal crimes are not confined to the page, you should hear the conversations they're having backstage |

|            |                                                                         |
|-----------:|-------------------------------------------------------------------------|
| **steve**  | Steve could you fill up my Evian bottle with more earth nectar, my vocal xylophones are as parched as a virgin's secret desert garden. |
| **poetri** | We're not opposed to all metaphors |
| **steve**  | Or comparisons it's just that getting caught with your similes exposed can be really embarrassing |
| **steve and poetri** | So, if you want your poems to stay so fresh and so clean (clean) sometimes its just better to say what you mean. |

# FIRST taste

*written by* **Beau Sia**

| beau | georgia me | suheir |
|---|---|---|
| At some point<br>We are all inspired<br>By something | (sings "Purple Rain") | She wrote, I was born a<br>black woman and have<br>now become a Palestinian |
| | Ever since I saw<br>Prince | Ever since I read<br>June Jordan |
| Growing up in<br>Oklahoma | | |
| Inspired me to write | Inspired me to write | Inspired me to write |
| (humming<br>"Oklahoma") | Why use words? Why<br>not music? How did<br>you infect me<br>with such writing desire? | Prose cut like diamonds |
| | Those little Corvette<br>Words Darling Nikki,<br>Get off type words | Your words made me<br>want to spread myself<br>open<br>    until all of me came<br>    out…to share with the<br>    world |
| Because of you my<br>Dear sweet skyline | | |
| Every shopping mall<br>Stampede | | |
| | Every breakthrough<br>video | |

| beau | georgia me | suheir |
|---|---|---|
|  |  | Everything I do in the dark<br>Every Broken hearted<br>stanza |
| Every seven eleven<br>Adventure<br>Every bowling alley<br>Dating fiasco | every crazy headline<br>every name change | whisper the words only<br>only poetry can be |
| Every self hating<br>Assimilated Asian | Every self hating<br>Assimilated Asian | Every self hating<br>Assimilated Asian |
| Has fueled my rant | Put freak glitter in<br>In my chants | adds meaning to my<br>simple Words |
| Carried under<br>suburban Sky | Into the stadium of<br>My heart | Where<br>Poetry is not a luxury |
| Oklahoma |  | June |
|  | Artist formerly known<br>As... |  |
| Your mullets gave me<br>Material |  | Your word was born in<br>this manufactured world. |

| beau | georgia me | suheir |
|---|---|---|
| | You made me so wet I had to start writing Poetry. | |
| Your touch has made… | | |
| | | Your touch |
| | Your touch has made the words | |
| Your touch has made The words fly from me Until they learned to Carry themselves | Your touch has made the words fly from me | Your touch has made the words fly… |
| | | They became my words |
| OKC…so much more | | |
| OOOOOOO | OOOOOOOOO | OOOOOOOOOOO |
| Than New York | | |
| | | June more |
| (The three give the poetry snaps) | | |
| | | than spoken word |
| | Prince you got more | |
| Uh | Uh Than James Brown | Uh |
| To give me other | Your fly doo and | Darwish, Audre Lorde |

30

| beau | georgia me | suheir |
|---|---|---|

**beau**

Reasons to rock. I
Don't want my children
Growing up afraid

**georgia me**

ass out showed me
where to take it.

**suheir**

Chrystos, Sapphire
Jimmy Santiago Baca,
Jayne Cortes

my words are
a flag.

My words are a
Reflection of
Possibility

My words are the
Shizzel my nizzel.

(Hums "Oklahoma")

| | My words | My words |
| | My words | My vulnerability |
| | My words | My growth |
| | My words | My joy |
| | My words | My chance |
| | My words | My truth |
| | My words | My gift |
| | My words | My self |

Prince

June Jordan

Oklahoma

Because of you
I write

Because of you
I write

Because of you
I write

# JAMMIN'

*written by* **Staceyann Chin** *and* **Black Ice**

**black ice**  Jam Master Jay
Was the man right here
He would stand right here
And command y'all attention

**staceyann**  Bob Marley was a prophet
ball player turned man with a mission
music was just the medium
a way to survive the tedium of small island life

**black ice**  The invention of the two turntables
and a mixer gave Jay purpose
when everyone said a black man's life was
worthless

**staceyann**  In these times
the death of our scribes
drives us to question the whys
the wherefores, the what do we lose when an artist
    dies

**black ice**  Jay had three kids and a wife
that's four reasons for life
and five reasons he should be here now
but he's not – so how
do we find the beauty in such an ugly set of circum-
    stances

**staceyann**  I remember when Bob crossed over
strangers crying in the streets
yawping sounds of riot and revolution
we sang redemption songs of freedom
of loss
we mourned him as a community
and were made whole

with every decomposition there is fertilization
for every empire that falls we witness
the birth of a new nation

**black ice**  This flower chopped off in full bloom
must become more than a tomb for other musicians
in his studio in Queens
his screams must be seen as more than just new
Nigga news
more than views spread among TV stations across
this nation
his passing must mean something in the grand
    scheme
of things

**staceyann**  When a man of the people dies
the skies open up to receive him
the sea sighs in anticipation of his arrival
the survival of the living
is deeply informed by the history of those dead
in legend Bob's locks are still flying
fingers still trying to resurrect
some version of Jimi Hendrix turned
John Coltrane turned nyabingi man

**black ice**  The Philly fresh fest
in memory still attests to Jay's talent
the balance of life and death
how the breath of those gone
is felt in the songs of those left singing

**staceyann**  We are ringing bells for Bob Marley

**black ice**  And Jam Master Jay

**black ice
and
staceyann**  For Aliyah
and Tupac and Marvin Gaye
These are some of the things we would say
if your bodies were still here with us today

# TITO Puente

*written by* **Lemon** *and* **Mayda Del Valle**

**lemon**  His last name meant bridge and his music gave us a way to crossover ask him if he played salsa and he would say

**mayda**  My music is not a sauce

**lemon**  He was the tenor of the timbal

**mayda**  The Don Corleone of Latin jazz

**lemon**  Played so well it looked like he was lip synching to the drum sticks

**mayda**  Invented the let out your tongue and play hard before Michael Jordan ever had hang time

**lemon**  Powdered white slickback round like a big mac phenomenal coke head

**mayda**  But you played that shit

**lemon**  Lived loved everything about the cun tun tun tun pra

**mayda**  You put 112th st. on the map

**lemon**  You made it El Barrio

**mayda and lemon**  You bad ass Boricua

**mayda**  You sniffed in mulattas and timbales

**lemon**  Toca coño toca

**mayda** You hit notes precise percussive sonidos of
Ran cun cun

**lemon** And you kept on never stopped

**mayda** Hands as fast as hummingbirds, spurred on a flurry
of wood against cowbells,

**lemon** And snare drums,

**mayda** Against cymbals,

**lemon** and skin stretched tight against metal bases

**mayda** You played oye como va mi ritmo... bueno para
gozar...

**lemon** For flags with no country, for latin, for jazz,

**mayda** for mambo, no salsa strictly pure old school
with a

**lemon** cun tun tun tun pra
kra kra pra tra ca ta

**mayda** for fierce latins
crossed borders
of nuyorican
and spic and English and music
Played with Machito, Mongo,

**lemon** and he gave Santana his first gold record...

**mayda** And dance, and rumba, and cha-cha-cha, and
guaguanco, and son, and swing

**lemon** and mambo

**mayda**   played jazz, played duke

**lemon**   and boogaloo

**mayda**   El Rey del Timbal

**lemon**   People danced for you Tito

| **mayda** | **lemon** |
|-----------|-----------|
| for drums | toca Tito toca |
| for dance | toca coño toca |
| for drums | toca Tito toca |
| for drums | toca coño toca |
| for dance | toca Tito toca |
| for drums | toca coño toca |
| for dance | toca Tito toca |

**mayda**   You played for dance Tito
You played high Tito
You made me high Tito

**lemon**   And higher

**mayda**   Tito!

**lemon**   And higher

**mayda**   Tito!

**lemon**   And higher

**mayda**   Tito!

**lemon and**   And you were our king!
**mayda**

# KRISPY KREME

*written by* **Poetri**

**poetri**  All I want to know is
Where did Krispy Kreme donuts come from?
What sick man invented this?
I see the sign every day!
'cause I'm in there every fricken day!
This black militant fella once told me
that Krispy Kreme
used to be called Krispy Kreme Kroissants...AHA!!!
Kroissant spelled with a K...
Just like the rest of their names
meaning KKK!
They were started to keep the black man
down and round
so when the revolution comes back around
all the black men would be too fat to fight,
going through withdrawal symptoms,
addicted to the KKK
made to order   glazed drugs...I mean donuts.

But everyday, I see white people inside
Krispy Kreme,
'cause I'm in there every fricken day!
I even saw the black militant fella'
in there one time
so I think it's safe to say that he was lying.
All the same Krispy Kreme is still trying to
kill me,
just like the KKK, the CIA and the devil

def poetry jam on broadway

Their stock has jumped leaps and bounds
since they met me
or should I say, since I met them
on that cold rainy night.
It was love at fist taste…
glaze melted into my mouth
like a waffle from Roscoes.
And I remember thinking in Shakespearean,
"What fresheth taste hath fallen
from grace into thine mouth."

They know me by a first name basis
when I come in,
I'm like NORM from CHEERS…"POETRI!!!!!"
When I go through the drive-through,
they know my voice,
"What's up, Poetri, the usual?"
"NO I DON'T WANT THE USUAL…
ALRIGHT GIVE ME THE USUAL!!!!!!"

I try to disguise my voice at times
and I think I'm pretty good,
You should hear my Fat Albert, but
they know it's me,
'cause I can only do fat people!
It's not fair, I already have
french fries I have to deal with,
now this!
I must forever fight the temptation,
of the creation of the perfect fattening donut…
Krispy Kreme!

# nig-gods

*written by* **Georgia Me**

**georgia me**  In celebration of all black men-Nig gods
N-I-G-G-O-D-S.
Real nigga's don't claim to be anything
they just are
who they are,
what they are, where they are; ghetto superstars
I love the way a nigga walks and talk
how he maneuvers when he gets caught
sheer poetry in motion when a nigga puts down game
ain't too many nigga's lame
maybe insane,
but only to those that can't understand
what it's like to be a Blackman
I love a nigga with sleepy eyes,
black lips, and toned thighs
the rumor ain't true for all
but I like a nigga wit' some size
but dick ain't what makes me fall
to me the mind is the prize
brothers who seek knowledge
didn't necessarily go to college
but those who are conscious of the true plan
who realize God is every black man
can I get an Amen?!!?
I'm your number one fan
from chocolate to caramel it all looks so sweet
visions of beauty as they walk down the street
head full of dreads, Tims on they feet;
they walk as if they're listening to a beat

Black men are the only creation
that command your attention on impact
by their color, their spirit, the way they act
as a matter of fact, I'm amazed
at how they handle situations
all across these nations
doors locking, purse watching,
looks of fear as they enter the station
but they laugh and move on,
steady grooving to a song
Fuck you cracker, I might be blacker
I'm God's reflection so fear me
you need protection
I ain't here to hate just to celebrate
my nigga's from that south
with them golds in their mouth
with them fingerwaves, fades and braids
forever pimpin' never ever getting played
my niggas from the west with them khakis and
    chucks
permed out creased down, fly as fuck
my nigga's from this east
that belly of the beast
surviving day to day never a moment of peace
if all my kings understood their power
they wouldn't waste a minute,
a second an hour on this bullshit
They want you to quit your journey
to find your spirit and to ignore your heart
to where you can't hear it
Nig-gods.

# SHINE

*written by* **Lemon**

**lemon**   This is for my people in jail
Where I learned to read and write poetry
…Etheridge Knight*

While white America sings about the
Unsinkable Molly Brown,
Tell me who was hustling the titanic when
that shit went down
I sing to thee of Shine the Stoker
who was hip enough to flee the fucking ship
and let the rich folks drown with screams
on their lIps
Jumped his black ass into the dark sea
Shine did broke free from the straining steel
I sing to thee of Shine and how the
millionaire banker stood on the deck
and pulled from his pocket a million dollar check
screaming— "Shine, Shine, save poor me,
and I'll give you all the money a black boy needs
and how Shine looked at the money
and then at the sea
and said "Jump in motherfucker and swim like me"
and Shine swam on, Shine swam on
and how the banker's daughter ran naked on the deck
with her pink tits trembling and her pants
around her neck
screaming— "Shine Shine, save poor me,
and I'll give you all the pussy a black boy needs."
and how Shine said
"pussy's good, and that's no jive,

def poetry jam on broadway

but you got to swim, not fuck to stay alive."
and Shine swam on. . . . Shine swam on . . .
and how Shine passed a preacher
floating on a board saying—
"Save me nigger Shine in the name of the Lord."
and how the preacher grabbed Shine's arm
and broke his stroke and how Shine pulled
out a shank and cut the preacher's throat
and Shine swam on, Shine swam on.
and when the news hit the shore
That the titanic had sunk
Shine was up in Harlem damn near drunk.

* from *The Essential Etheridge Knight*, published University of Pittsburg Press, 1986

# SHE

*written by* **Steve Colman**

**steve**  She loved to
dance so much
it was a habit
she did the butterfly
the pop lock
and rocked the
Roger Rabbit
She wore FuBu and Phat Farm
She had a "thug life" tattoo
scratched into the rough skin
on her right arm
She watched MTV
for the rap video action clips
and the fashion tips
She wore Polo cologne
less for the guys
than for the passing 'chicks'
She worshipped Biggie
and cried
when Tupac got lost
She thought that
Will Smith was too soft
She bought the StarTac mobile phone
for when her soldiers roamed
She took the bus to work
as a barback at the Bennigans
by the mobile homes
She memorized
complex rhyme schemes
like

walking by
gave me this awkward eye
in the parking lot
with his Karl Kani
and told her friends
if Eminem can do it
then so can I
She ignored the boys
in the park
who told her 'girls can't rhyme'
She tagged her name
on her high school's classroom walls
and battled other Emcee's
in the bathroom stalls
until her voice went hoarse
She read the Rap Pages
and dreamed
about a five mic review
in the Source

But when she graduated
her dreams faded
just another emcee
who never made it
so she traded her FuBu and Tag
for a blue suit and a badge
She became a security guard
like her dad
She switched the mic spit
to the night stick
exchanged the tight clique
for the night shift
at Rickels and Daffy Dans

She sold nickel bags of weed
for extra cash
from the back seat of her cousin's crappy van
She had twin baby boys
and an order of protection
from an abusive man

What happens to a rhyme deferred?
Does it dry up
while you're a raising a son?
Or does it expose
the closed fists
and broken dishes?
What happens when
you meet the genie
but you can't make the wishes?
When your hands demand an object
that your fingers can't reach
When the pot of gold
is a promise
that the rainbow can't keep

# LONE SOLDIER

*written by* **Black Ice**

**black ice**  My father always told me
I'd understand
When I got older
This internal hurt
of a lone soldier
so
held firmly in my right
arm
with her head on my
shoulder, cause that's the way she likes me
to hold her
that's what I told her...

speaking about my daughter
in order to
save face
because
just before the embrace
and all the
"I love you's"
and
"I miss you's"
she clearly let me know
she had issues...

Talkin' about
"Daddy where you been?"
and just then
my mind began
sinking back

thinking back
to those
Saturday seldom show up days
Those
Seems like my father
don't wanna bother
helping me grow up days

so sick of not seeing
my dad
I
Wanna throw up days
Those
My mom said
"don't come nowhere near,
where we resided
'cause she decided to
blow up days"…

Well, anyways,
Her eyes were always
able to
pull the disguise
off any lies
I might try to use
to summarize
the situation.
It's funny the way
It's second nature
The way I put these
words to paper
But
couldn't figure out
a simple explanation
to offer my baby girl

Don't like having to
admit
That tomorrow's just
a maybe girl
Or
The famous
"Ask your mom, and
see what she says."
But the ball's
in her court
so we gotta play
how she plays
But hey...

I tell my big girl
not to fret
'Cause all that's dirty
will come out
in life's wash
and
We haven't finished
filling up yet

You see,
when two parents
are not in conjunction
a dysfunctional child
is inevitable
see,
mommy's not on time with daddy
daddy's not on time with mommy
So,
The child grows up
Off schedule

# daddy's SONG

*written by* **Suheir Hammad**

**suheir**  You always loved classics
Said new music was shit
Just like comedians couldn't make
Jokes without getting nasty no more
Singers couldn't sing

In your day there was Sinatra Presley
You hated him – wouldn't let us watch
His flicks and some cat named Cooke

All the time Sam Cooke could sing Sam
Cooke sang real songs simple and good

I was in high school the first time I heard
Your mix tape of Cooke classics and I fell
In love with that voice smooth smooth.
And I fell in love with the Daddy I thought
All this time talking about some Sinatra
Presley like guy not this sweet
Sweet music.

I was in college when we rented
Malcolm's life on video and maybe the best
Thing Spike Lee ever did was play
That song, your song, as Malcolm
I mean Denzel was getting ready to die
You cried in your easy boy
Reclining your head to better listen

That was you daddy born
By a river in a little tent and I
Swear you've been running ever since.

That's my song too Daddy
And one day I'm going to
Sing it for you in a poem.

# music piece

*written by* **The Company**

**company**    (whispering) Hip-hop, Hip-Hop, Hip-Hop. . . . (cont.)
(Mayda joins in with a rhythmic chant. Lemon joins in with high hat sounds. Poetri with Lemon, whispers an underscore of the word "Poetry." Beau joins in after eight measures with human break beat. Four measures later Steve comes in with the first verse. The music continues under the verses.)

**steve**    It's like this ———and a
It's like that ———and a
It was poetry, but now they call it rap—and a
Before playas hustlas
gangstas crooks
it was Gil Scott-Heron and Gwendolyn Brooks
before books and presses
printed all our lessons
it was griots on the corner
spittin' with a message
the gift is a blessin' and the
blessin' let me see
That you're blind, baby, you're blind
to the fact that —

**georgia me**    I never knew that I could be free
until this music came to me and saved me
told me to look beneath the lies
always ask why why the cries
show that tries succeed through this

spoken word I must feed like
Tupac, Goodie Mob, Nas and Chuck D
Do it so all God's people get freed

**staceyann** (yells) Rewind!!!!

> (Music stops. Tendaji joins with a
> beat-box reggae beat. The remaining
> company, join follow his vibe.)

Now my journey to this hip hop trip
began with the beat, the base on some
reggae tip
quick—Flip it around, turn it upside down
bubble your pot like a dance hall queen
from downtown
Trenchtown—No joke
spoken word is about to leave
the ground—like a plane—chain
ganging, clanging like a school boy with a pan
understand
Jamaican, American
we all part of this Big Bumbo Raas Claat Plan

> (The music stops once more, and
> the company changes the beat.)

**black ice** We are
the inherent carriers
of the
words of the Earth
see
we've been destined to
do this shit
since birth

and
for what it's worth
y'all call us
poets
and
you and I know it
we're hot
but see
featured or not
we don't switch our plot
while
other cats who
claim our vibe
use their scribe
for superficial
and selfish needs
see
when upon the mic
our soul bleeds
life's lessons
taught to us
through our own
indiscretions
and
understood
through our ancestors
blessings
and
Hip
Hop.

**lemon**   Children playing, women producing
Men go work and some go stealin'
Everyone's got to make a living.

END OF ACT ONE.

# act two

## the stuff
## DREAMS ARE
## made of

*written by* **The Women**

**staceyann**   Butterflies…

**suheir**   Phenomenal…

**mayda**   Exquisite…

**georgia me**   Hallelujah…

**staceyann**   Write me a love poem
Use me pretty words like
Butterflies
Say something powerful

**georgia me**   Like vagina

**staceyann**   Fuck it, I need you say pussy

**chorus**   Pussy

**staceyann**   Whisper those kinds of words across my belly

**georgia**   Talk political about my feet

**staceyann**   Tell me it cannot be wrong
To want you.

**chorus**   Such dreams I have.

**staceyann**   Of our children
They will be…
Gods among us

**suheir**   Poems written for you lover…

**mayda**   Sister

| | |
|---|---|
| **georgia me** | Warrior |
| **staceyann** | Woman, sing those words to me |
| **staceyann** | Butterflies… |
| **suheir** | Phenomenal… |
| **mayda** | Exquisite… |
| **georgia me** | Hallelujah… |
| **mayda** | I miss your nook. The way we fit from the very first night |
| **georgia me** | I miss more the way<br>You want me to hold you. |
| **chorus** | Help me believe. |
| **mayda** | I am bigger<br>Than my 5'1" mini wonder woman frame<br>Holding your rough, |
| **georgia me** | Your stubble |
| **suheir** | Lean limbs |
| **staceyann** | Long eyelashes |
| **mayda** | Against my impatience and passion<br>Let me warm you a plate |
| **suheir** | Just how you like it. |
| **mayda** | And show you it doesn't come from submission<br>But caring for you…I feel like |
| **chorus** | I can fix the world. |
| **mayda** | When I hold you<br>I believe I am made of something stronger |

| | |
|---|---|
| **georgia me** | I am in existence because of this dream |
| | I am from He or She |
| **mayda** | Whatever you need God to be |
| **georgia me** | You can allow destruction |
| | To reign with a simple refrain of |
| **chorus** | It ain't my problem |
| **georgia me** | In this world we are lost soldiers at war |
| | With rank and no commanding |
| **staceyann** | Fallen prey to the demanding day to day |
| **georgia me** | Grinding all night to make that pay |
| **chorus** | Walking blind in daylight |
| **georgia me** | Can't find a way |
| | Recognize . . . we have strayed |
| **chorus** | Strayed away from love. |
| **suheir** | In a poem composed of touches and glances |
| **chorus** | In the silence |
| **suheir** | Between heartbeats |
| **chorus** | The stuff dreams are made of |
| **suheir** | Is love the smell |
| **chorus** | Behind my ear |
| **suheir** | The aura |
| **chorus** | Round my rear |

| | |
|---|---|
| **staceyann** | The way a woman walks |
| **georgia me** | Legs solid as stalks |
| **mayda** | Of orchid of dahlia |
| **suheir** | Of Earth we |
| **staceyann** | Break down |
| **mayda** | Dance |
| **georgia me** | And give birth. |
| **suheir** | To laughter, to rapture, to possibility.<br>The stuff dreams are made of is all of me. |
| **staceyann** | Butterflies... |
| **suheir** | Phenomenal... |
| **mayda** | Exquisite... |
| **georgia me** | Hallelujah... |
| **staceyann** | Butterflies... |
| **suheir** | Phenomenal... |
| **mayda** | Exquisite... |
| **georgia me** | Hallelujah... |
| **staceyann** | Butterflies... |
| **suheir** | Phenomenal... |
| **mayda** | Exquisite... |
| **georgia me** | Hallelujah... |

# LOVE POEMS

*written by* **Lemon**

**lemon**   Love poems
shit love poems don't pay the fuckin' rent
you got to come stronger than that baby
you got to come stronger than that
but then you know maybe it's just me
playing this role like my heart is cold
I figure if you don't know
then you're never gonna know
that yeah I did love somebody one time
what I took this little girl from a shorty
and turned her into a fly ass dime
and when I thought she was mine
all mine nobody else's but mine
it wasn't even like that jack
sometimes when I think back
I feel a little guilty
'cuz, you know, I step to her
when she was nothing but a Similac
I had to see where her head was at
and that's when I knew
she was gonna grow up and be all that
matter of fact till this day
ain't no girl out there got more props than her
Nah cause you see my little love
had a way of looking up to me
like I was her big brother
taking care of me and feeding me like she was my
    mother

and everything we ever did in this world
seem to be original cause we was each other's first
    lovers
so there's no other girl out there with more props
    than her
plus I don't even see myself going through that again,
    my friends
I guess that's why I have a hard time
writing love poems
'cuz I love love
but I like to leave love where its at pure
just like that
no added preservatives
no trying to run it through a test
just leave it alone and let it manifest
'cause its bad enough the truth already suffers
from too much analysis
and ain't nothing more truer than love.

ain't nothing more painful either I ain't joking
I'd rather catch an ass whooping
than get my heart broken
'cause an ass whooping will come quick
depending how many are giving it to you of course
but a broken heart
a broken heart will work its up in you nice and slow
and before you know you're laying on your living floor
talkin' bout I don't want to live no more
memories of my little love
got me in the zone
but I still ain't writin'
no fuckin' love poems.

# HOOD DAYS

*written by* **Mayda Del Valle**

**mayda** While Ricky's livin la vida loca
I'm sitting at home in front of my TV living la vida sola

wishing this thing called love came with a handbook
'cause its getting to the point where I'm getting so
cold-hearted and bitter
my heart's freezing over and I'm giving Frigidare some
competition

wishing I could go back to school days
when love could be as simple as writing a note
decorated with hearts and flowers
or is friends saying
"pssst pssst
he told me to tell you he likes you . . ."
and you picked the petals off of flowers to decide the
fate of:
He loves me, He loves me not

Yea
you know them  days
those hopscotch, BMX bikes, double dutch and roller
skate days
those peanut butter and jelly sandwiches and Tang in
a glass jar days
those getting dressed up just to walk down the block
and see your crush days

those chasing after the soft serve ice cream trucks
   and opening the fire hydrant
to turn your curbside into a pool on hot summer days
those after school videos followed by
Voltron, Inspector Gadget, He-Man, GI-Joe
hey yoooooo Thundercats
and
She-Ra's really He-Man's sister days?

those
*can it be that it was all so simple* days?
when love's ways were so easily understood
I long for those childhood days
in my hood
when smiling up at the hot sun blaze in your face
meant
today was a good day

but we run away from childhood simplicity
striding quickly
into playing games where we tag each other's hearts
   with our own insecurities
losing sense of life's possibilities
and wondering
how the time went by so quickly.

# litany
# OF DESIRE

*written by* **Staceyann Chin**

**staceyann**   Her body is a litany of desire
And I
Wrap them frail around
My body
Ribs striped and stretched

                          Toward healing

  grotesque
  beautiful
  these sores
I carry them
fingers sticky and heavy with exactitude
I flay the muscled sacrament
with wine
and water
and bread
and worship
I want you
litany
like bleeding
like a fire fanned open
like my legs
insistent
like fate
like salt
like memory

    tell    them to me

                your stories
        tender to the touch
                this
is what I have always wanted
                        from you
the cracked edge
of what has
just
                begun to harden
I want you
against time
and revelation
and beds too far away
I want you wanting me
clothed in the absolution
of fangs and forks and fucks we shouldn't have
I want you
buried in the belly of a blind belief
like Jonah
like apostle
like Mary
and Joseph
        like God
I want your spirit
        made flesh
                within me
        frail
and futile
        I want to follow you
broken ground you
    sound you
hoarse from the flick
of this foreign tongue

like mud
and martyr
and mornings without sun
I want to quiet you
like quick
like cunt
like hollow
   like whole
—I want to hold you
holy
like prayer
like benediction
like intercession
like hallelujah, like hallelujah,
like hallelujah
like    amen.

# DATING MYSELF

*written by* **Poetri**

**poetri**  Everywhere I go I see ugly people
with cute people,
and I can't help to ask myself
what does she see in that guy?
inner beauty? Well, I have a whole lot of that
I see these happy couples and I used to think
what do I have to do to get a girl
like that?
Then that evolved into
what do I have to do to get a girl?

Now, I'm exhausted from thinking.
fatigued from trying to convince myself
that I'm worthy of another being,
tired of looking but not really looking
so it doesn't appear that I'm desperate
weary of being afraid to tell someone
that I'm interested,
in fears that they will avoid me
consumed from being alone
no longer will I be at the mercy of
ladies to like me,
no longer will I be trying to look
my best for women
that don't know that I'm
in love with them.

nmore oh!!!

Yes from now on I am dating myself!

I already talk to myself
so I know my conversations will be good
I've always said that I wanted to be with
someone that's just like me.
well there's no one more like me than me
it's not like I'm dating my cousin or nothing
I looked it up,
there's nothing in the law books
that say a man can't date himself
I don't know why I didn't think of this before
I amaze myself, sometimes
I laugh and joke with myself
on lonely days praying
hard for better days.
now we can get through the rough
times together.

no one to impress but myself

I probably still will play games
with myself
cry with myself, lie to myself
'cause I'd hate to hurt myself's feelings
I'll only be looking out for myself, though.

but, you know how women are
once they see you with someone
all of a sudden now they want to get with you!
all of a sudden I'm that cute guy
that is dating someone now.

I assure you I'm not doing this to make
other women jealous
I am completely happy with myself
I like myself
I mean I think I am attractive!
I plan to be with myself 'til the very end
or until someone
better comes along

# BUT

*written by* **Steve Colman**

**steve**   This is the first love poem I ever wrote
so I'm going to need some help from the audience
you'll know where to jump in
it's called "My Lover's Sorry But."

My lover almost always said 'but'
at the end of I love you
after dinner after sex after work after noon after a
    while
all I heard was, 'I love you, but'
I love you, but
what about your brother
I'll never be number one to you
I love you, but
I want to travel by myself
I want to teach English in Ecuador Guatemala
    Madagascar
I love you, but
you like Taco Bell
and I want to live on a commune
and grow organic vegetables
in fields that we fertilize with our recycled shit
while reading 1001 ways to save the planet
by candlelight
I love you, but . . .
my lover loved but

so much
that her but grew bigger everyday
pushing me into a dark corner
in the rear of the room
I shared
with my lover
and her but
and so now
I'm leaving her…But
behind

# LOVE

*written by* **Beau Sia**

**beau**  I think that love is the most beautiful
Thing in the world
And I don't give a fuck.
'Cuz I have no original ideas.
to get women to fall in love with me
Women who hear this
Fall in love with me !

'Cuz that's what it comes down to.
Life or death

I've seen a man
Jack off to a Gap window display
So don't tell me love isn't important.
But, love isn't that easy
In fact, love is
the bane of my existence
The reason why I hate
Valentine's Day and Halloween,
Which is about ghosts
and I think you know where
I'm going here.
I'm going to the land
And maybe
I've only got 3 ghosts
in this land
But that doesn't mean they don't bring their friends,
'Cuz girls rarely travel alone
in this land

Lydia is from this land.

I used to kiss her while listening to
The Cure's just like heaven

Now that song makes me sad.

Why must we associate music
With our love lives?
I'm not trying to be profound here,
I'm just saying that music takes me back

And I can't explain the memory
Process involved in that,
Because I was not a psychology major
And maybe my problem
With picking up college age women
Has to do with me always asking
"Yo' shorty, What's your major?"

Maybe I shouldn't think of women
in terms of picking up them up
and maybe I should open up my
sensitive side
but really the sensitive side sucks
I've been there
you can only imagine
the kinds of sweaters they make you wear.
It's not fair. Love is not fair
And war is not fair
I don't care what anybody has to
say about that.
I feel unloved.

Am I the only one?
I know I can't be that misunderstood
But you don't want to
understand me
you just want to hear the part about
my small dick again
'cuz the Asian man
will always be plagued by this
rumor until he is brave enough to whip it out on stage
and say
"Ha! We are gigantic."

Honestly, this is not the direction
I wanted to take this poem

I just want to be in the arms of
my true love,
in a wonderful, perfect
world with our two children
Helga and Lamar,

'cuz love
has got me fucked up and dying
and I feel retardo
without anyone to hold me
and maybe that's sentimental
but what's wrong with sentimental

All I'm saying is someone love me.

# KEEP THE FAITH

*written by* **Black Ice**

**black ice**  Have you ever...
Been with the one you love
And
All alone at the same moment
In time?
Layin' with your back
Against cold cadavers
Filled with
Dead emotions that
Refuse to understand
Your frame of mind
When the strain of time has
Taken its toll
and gaining control is our only goal
selfishly in conjunction where
the things I used to say
to make you laugh and smile
have now become major malfunction
with the one you love and
all alone at the same moment in time
where
wounds run deep
in painful streams of denial
that make happiness a crime
where relaxing mid Sunday love sessions
turn into frustrating late night Monday
masturbation
misunderstanding distorts

so sarcastic retorts
become our only conversation
no communication and
mis-interpretation have us
constantly passing the buck
so when I'm with the one I love
and actually in love
and wanna make love
she just thinks I wanna fuck
when the omnipresent beauty
of our love
seems to need a complete
makeover
where our undivided attention
has become distracted
and
mistrust and deceitful thinking
take over
and rake over genuine feelings
of unconditional co-existence
when the silence seems golden
but it's actually brass underneath
it's passive resistance
lack of persistence
and no assistance
into getting to the root of the debate
has us listenin' to love songs
we just sang together the other day
the other day swearing we can't relate
we hate this fate
that seems to await us
but believe it to be
the ultimate outcome

but
Sis…
that's when we must dig deep
inside ourselves
to hear that ever constant shout
from our souls allowing the spirit
to open up and visualize the faith
that the physical eyes
cannot make sight of
because although I'm overwhelmed
with loneliness … shit…
I'm with the one I love
at the same moment in time
just overdosing
on egotistical anesthetics
numbing my emotions
so the love only seems sublime.
We gotta
keep the faith…..

# hit like A MAN

*written by* **Georgia Me**

**georgia me**  Hit like a man, let them know you're a man
put all your power behind that fist
you're the ruler of this land and as
the sand falls through the hour glass
I hope this love lasts and
all the pain surpasses
tired of the lashes,
bruises I tell others are rashes
oh the sunglasses cover the eye
but baby my lip
I told my mama I stumbled and tripped
she thinks I'm clumsy
or take too many sips of the wine
which inclines me to feel fine
eases the humiliation
of how you beat my behind
I know you're under pressure
from work and the world
but please watch how you hit me
in front of our little girl
she doesn't understand this abuse her father
feeds
there's no believable excuse
the truth in my eyes she reads
in her eyes I see disappointment and confusion
she shed tears over the broken limbs
and severe contusions
I want our family so I choose not to leave
tired of being thrown like a rag doll
by my sleeve

sick by the situation so I constantly heave
I can't make her believe this is love I receive
it's a hard pill to swallow
with this program I just can't follow
I'm starting to believe your heart is hollow
or full of hate
hoping it will get better so I wait
praying stupidity isn't an inheritable trait
for I don't want our daughter to live a life
of cover-ups and cries
standing before a judge giving feeble alibi's.
Loving a man so much she loses herself
hating herself so much
she gives a damn about her health
for who wants to live just to suffer
pain is inevitable, it only makes you tougher
but suffering is optional and I've made my choice
for my little girl, I'm her hero
her example, and her voice
I will not allow her future to be a replay
of my existence
I had to break free from this jail,
end my life sentence
I tried to go quietly but you slapped me in my face
kicked me in the stomach, ripped my dress,
and out my mouth you slapped the taste
As I got up from the floor
I stared you in your eyes and realized
the burning hell brewing on the inside
knowing there could be no place I could run or hide
my only escape would be your utter demise
I can't hit like a man
and I hate to pull the trigger
but let your life be a lesson
for all those pussy ass niggas.

# WE SPENT the
## *4th of July In Bed*

*written by* **Suheir Hammad**

**suheir**   Even now walking girls
are exploding legs stepping
on shells of American hatred
left dug in Iraqui soil
Even now Malaysian girls
choose between the sex trade and hunger
Phillipinas go blind constructing
the computer discs poems like this
are saved on

Even now lover as we lay
in amazement and if baby
as you say my skin is the color of sun warmed
sand then you're my moonless night
and we the beach wet tidal
all that good ssshhhh
wet yet as we lay

Shrapnel awakens pain on an
island of young paraplegics courtesy
of the '80s gun craze

To our generation violence isn't a phase
it's the day
to day and though my head is filled
with your sweetness now this same
head knows Nagasaki girls picked

maggots out of stomach sores
with chopsticks Hiroshima mothers rocked
headless babies to sleep

This head knows Palestinian youth
dead absorbing rubber bullets
homes demolished trees
uprooted roots dispersed

This same head with all them
love songs and husky whispers

knows our touch is not free
it comes with responsibility

Even as we lay in all this good
feeling people lay in dirt vomit
shit and blood
and I gotta tell you
that my sincere love for real is
for my peeps my family humanity`
love for real freedom
well fed human dignity

Lover even now I open myself
to share this I gotta tell you
there ain't enough good feeling
to push the pain and awareness
out not enough nothing to
make me forget and I ain't
no woman of steel it feels
needed this kiss that
touch there that rhythm

needed and wanted
hold me a little while longer
just a bit, just a bit
'Cause we gotta get up soon
Come on now baby
we got work to do.

# A TOAST

*written by* **Lemon**

**lemon**   This is not about the murderers, the convicts
The three time loser, the first time felon
or the skidbidder
This is not about the C.O.'s the wardens,
The commissary
The crips, the bloods, the kings
Or how much time you got on the phone homey
This is not about the D.A. or the legal aid
'cuz after they're done railroading your ass up north
they go to lunch together anyway
This poem is as priceless as a carton of
cigarettes
and a brand new pair of creased greens
This is a toast
to freedom
just cause you locked up
don't mean you can't be free
matter of fact the first day of your bid
the options are available
the doors wide open
you could be Muslim
and sing a song to raise the sun
you could be 5 percent
and understand that the mathematics
behind the language of kimetic is that... it is...
the original tongue of man my brother
you could be Christian and go from
being Catholic to being confused
to knowing the only way is to fear God
and you got nothing to lose

everything to gain
can I get a witness...
you could be a Nazi and hate all of the above
but we don't get much of those around here
plus the Israelites will set that ass straight
but you got to believe in something
or you will be a rhythmless void
so here's a toast to my God and all of y'all
who play the yard
May your word be born and may you find
that the Lord may not come when you call
but he's always on time.

# **descandancy**

*written by* **Mayda Del Valle**

**mayda**  It's nice . .
that you can claim your clan to purebred pedigree
    descendancy
but middle passages mark the makeup of my
    amalgamated
Afro-Boricua ancestry.
I know it's kinda hard to see the motherland
    legitimacy in me
but I can't deny the fact that Youruba songs
lay in the lines of my mother's palms
as
offerin' up Psalms
seekin' the calm offered by God's son
'cause
when the day is done
the color of my skin still
marks me as an alien in the country of my birth.
I can't check myself into a box
I'd be ignoring mami's straight and papi's nappy locks
    in me
the chi-town Midwest windy city me
the be-bop
hip-hop
non-stop
salsa con sabor
queen of soul in me
the growing up next door to mexicanos
with
Orale cabrones
tacos and tamales in me

*def poetry jam on broadway*

The descendancy that doesn't deny the darker
    shades of skin in me
the what in me
yes the THAT in me
what you claim you can't see
so descend and see
descend and see me for what I be
'cause I be a Rican
a Chi-town not a Nuyorican
a Chi-town south-side Rican simply seekin' to see if I
    can fit in
I dare you to still in your chair and
intellectualize what I can only make sense of by
    feelin'
I see
you're being blind not seein' past the kinds of
    fabricated fictional fables
assaulted ancestral accounts
I should be callin' your historical scribes Aesop
the way they stop
the truth from being illuminated
using tactics
Trying to force my assimilation
'causin' me to question my creation
You must've mistaken me for Hansel and Gretel
thinkin' I'd jump into the meltin' pot
always trying to place me in constant categorizations
    of populations
You calling this shit civilization?


My so-called pre-Columbian savage
unenlightened ancestors
had more humanity

than your Microsoft
Macintosh technology
Monopoly information highway riding bareback
on the backs of underpaid third world women and
    children
85 cents a day for makin' hundred dollar nike's
nuclear bomb droppin'
immigrant stoppin'
death by lethal electrocution
injectin'-lies-of-let-me-get-my-piece-of-the-American-
    apple-pie-dream-into-our-children's-minds society
LET ME order your new world and paint the White
    House brown coz
I'M GOING DOWN
yes I'm goin' down to the earth searchin' my roots
    like Hailey's
and I'm ridin' comets back to the past
back to the past that becomes my future that is my
    present that is my now
I'm goin' back seekin'
My Descendancy

# MONEY

*written by* **Poetri**

**poetri**  My money has been acting funny lately
all I ever did was love her!
maybe too much!
'cause now it's like we ain't cool no more

I got more than a hunch she's playing me
trying to make me jealous,
hanging out with other fellas
always in some other brother's pocket!

I try and tell her those other guys
are just using her!
"They just using you money!!!"
she don't wanna hear me
she won't even return my phone calls!
she doesn't even stop by the crib like she used to
she won't go to the movies with me
she won't even go get nothing to eat!
and you know a brother can't eat...without money!

there's only so much bread and water I can take.
call me spoiled, I remember the days
when people used to see us at the hottest clubs
the expensive restaurants,
all the high priced stores
I made sure I looked good with money!
I treated you right! I never abused you!

Did I? Money, did I abuse you?
did I get used to you hanging around and

now you're giving me a taste of what it
feels like to live without you?
People still think we're tight
they still ask about you.

Ever since Money hasn't been around
I feel like I'm losing my other friends too
American Express, Visa, Discover,
now they're acting starting to act shady!
I think she's spreading lies on me!
I tell you
I don't know what I did
but my money's been acting funny lately
and I don't know her anymore
and my life ain't the same
never will be the same
until Money comes back into my life
so if you see her or any of her cousins
let her know that I miss her
I love her, and I want her to come home.

# PASSING

*written by* **Staceyann Chin**

**staceyann**   Downtown Brooklyn is easy for me
long sheer skirts do little to hide
my open legged stride
see-through, button down sleeveless blouses
hug my bodice
so tight my nipples are barely concealed
by the carefully chosen push up bra from Macy's

see I'm a femme
so I can pass
the way our yellow skinned grandmothers passed
to escape the fields of cotton and sugarcane
   sweetened by black blood and sweat
they had to hide their blackness against the whip
and the rape and all the reasons that make us so
   afraid to live in the castle of our skins

the story is the same at Jay-street-borough-hall
when someone realizes a
young boy is really a young girl
and the red, white, and blue jacket
is not enough
to cover the tattoo on her belly
two naked women wrapped around each other
like pretzels that came out different
from the rest

it takes them two minutes to break two ribs
one for her lover who passes all the time

the other makes her grow
because now she knows she can never pass
she knows that butch bodies are too strong

too strange, too dark like those bronze bodies
that smell too thickly of rebellions
and revolutions
and we know revolutions take time
and sacrifice and lives to turn this world
all the way around
sometimes
it makes me angry that they think
I look like them
so they can convince themselves that
I am okay
but I hasten to show them the tangled
wool between my thighs,
the funk that rises from me only when my woman
touches me
I do not wish to pass
as almost straight
or nearly normal
holding down corporate jobs
stroking narrow minded dicks
so I can be invited to family dinners
so I can disown our brothers and sisters who cannot
    pass

we need to let them know that long
after these broken bones have healed
that we will still be here
and long after our bruised hearts no longer

hurt, we will still be here
and long long after our mothers no longer
weep
we will still be here
still gay, still black, still human
still surviving in the face of this blatant bigotry
that will one day force us to lace arms
so we can all strike back.

# SISTA TO sista

*written by* **Georgia Me**

**georgia me**  Why must you show yo' ass
why not have some class
do you wanna be lusted after
or respected
and ya wonder why real niggaz
reject ya
you ever wonder what a sista be thinkin'
when she in da club shakin' her ass drinkin'
drinkin' and shakin' till her ass is fucked up
but then she stuck when she luck up on
a nigga that just don't care
he wanna cut her up
and pull out dat hair
she wears a blond weave teased about four feet
styled in a fan
got it done by a nigga she claiming her man
but if she got a man why she in a club
letting niggaz molest her ,
she thinks that shit's love
it's not love, it's lust
but she wants that attention
she needs it from men
never knew her daddy had to mention
that's a clue to why a real nigga she never knew
with her loveless self,
there's no telling for a man
what she'll do
she'll shake, she'll smile, she'll lie,

she'll fuck
she'll drop, she'll lick
she'll swallow, she'll suck
niggaz can see this by her demeanor
he shows her some interest so she's eager
he's not concerned about how to please her
he'll use her even though her

resources are meager damn schemer
but when you act like a ho' you get pimped
you being played for a fool, a sucker, a simp
letting those fake niggaz
blow you up like a blimp
he'll never want you for his queen just a temp
now take that sixty dollars to the Pink Fox
and get your weave crimped
look at ya
buying clothes just to impress
people who aren't of good character
paying $140.00 for an outfit
when you make $200.00
that's a factor your priorities are all wrong

Well think about the cost of freezing
waiting an hour and a half to get in at Club 559
with a skirt right below your butt cheeks
sista's shake they head
brothers holla "FREAK"
"If you ain't cuttin' I ain't speakin'"
he ain't speakin' unless you freakin'
he'll hook up with you next weekend
to sit and chat and spit some game

you like him and figure "hey he's not a lame"
so you fuck him and don't even know his full name
when he doesn't call back you feel ashamed
I've been there my sista I feel your pain.
Sista to sista.

# mic CHECK

*written by* **Suheir Hammad**

**suheir**   Mic check 1
2 can you hear me mic
check 1-2

Mike checked my bags
at the airport in a random routine check

I understand Mike, I do
You too were altered that day
and most days
most folks operate on fear
often hate
this is mic check your job
and I am always random

I understand it was folks
who looked, smelled maybe
prayed like me

can you hear me Mike?
red cheeked with blonde buzz
cut with corn flower
eyes and a cross
round your neck

Mike check
folks who looked like you
stank so bad the Indians smelled them

mic check before they landed
they murdered 1-2 1-2
as they prayed,
spread small pox as alms

Mic check yes I
packed my own bags
can you hear me no
they have not been out of my possession

Thanks Mic you have a good day too
1-2 check Mike can you hear me
hear me check Mic
Hey yo, Mike, who's gonna check you?

# TERRORIST THREAT

*written by* **Steve Colman**

**steve**  There's a terrorist threat in America
And we can barely accept
It' scary that our country's been
Wrecked by barbarians
Derelict clerics
With exotic names like
Trent Lott and Kathleen Harris
I'm going to Paris
Because they killed democracy in Florida
Quick call the coroner

There's been a hostile takeover of
Of the red white and blue
They finance corporate mergers
So when Enron and congress fuck
Everybody gets screwed

They're holding hostages
In hot factories overseas
They torture their victims
With long hours and slave wages
They crave little girls
Mostly southeast Asian and Haitian
I've seen the videotapes
So R. Kelly isn't the only one
Who should be charged with
Child molestation

There is a terrorist threat in the land
and it's not just the boy bands
They have a plan
it's inherited through history
they destroyed the native tribes
now each July they celebrate their victory
instead of making things more equal
they build prisons for poor people
pass petty bids and life sentences
to kids selling weed and other sedatives
but they disregard the evidence
when they select a rich white boy from Texas
and declare a crackhead President

There's a terrorist threat in the nation
they give tax breaks to big banks
but deny black people reparations

They maintain training ranches
and congregate in klans
they steal Alaska's oil
Tally Bans
and censor art for sport
they snuck into our law schools and
hijacked the Supreme Court
Their money makes missiles
their labs created Anthrax.
Osama was their pawn
Evil is their axis

They're skilled at killing
innocent civilians
because they've had lots of practice

From Hanoi to Nicaragua
from Vieques to Damascus
for agua and oil
gold zinc and soil

They spread their views
on cable news
They call each other
George and Dick and Rudy
So next time you see a terrorist
kick him in his booty
it's not only your right
as an American
it's your patriotic duty.

# THE ASIANS ARE COMING, THE ASIANS ARE COMING

*written by* **Beau Sia**

**beau**   Look asshole, *Crouching Tiger ... Dragon*
was not our one shot at love
it's the pre cursor of what's to come
Oh yeah, now it's cool to like these Asian people
as long as they're being Asian on the big screen
and you set it in Asia, and it's a long time ago
and they're speaking in Asian (Thank God for
subtitles)
who cares if they're kissing?
as long as they're only kissing other Asians
you have nothing to worry about right?

Wrong motherfucker
we're not just on the big screen
in the kung fu flicks you adore
we are everywhere

we are programming your websites
making your executives look smart
and getting into your schools for free

raise the bar and we'll meet it

and we're not just kissing other Asians

our mad sexy asses are getting play all
over the ethnic spectrum

how the fuck do you think Tiger Woods,
Rob Schneider, and Keanu Reeves were made?
that's right.
The Asian invasion is a reality and
we fuck so good
it's only gonna get bigger

bigger than play station 2,
Tae Kwon Do, curry, yoga,
and sister in laws,
you asked for a global economy
well so sorry
if it blows up in your face and goes beyond
getting a billion Chinese on AOL

eating KFC in their Gap khakis

Am I ranting? Fuck yeah
and you're not shutting me up until
the egg roll is recognized as an American
food
So, rise up
let's give America the melting pot
it's always talked about
and watch hair get darker
eyes get smaller
and everyone fuck that much better.

# FRONT page

*written by* **Black Ice**

**black ice**  Oh damn
That's that cat that changed his name
from David to Ayatollah
High roller
Motorola soldier tech nine under his
Polar
Ass nigga
Don't know his future from past nigga
But that fast trigger got this die cast
Forty ounce swigger thinking his shit
Is bigger than mine
It's not surprising to find that your state of mind got
    you parking that 63 thousand dollar Lex you flex
Right outside your mother's hard earned 22,000
    dollar duplex you know, the one right next to the
    projects
Where pseudo elated coke gang created
Crime related manhood got you assed out nigga
Getting high to you pass out nigga
Quick way up fast way out nigga
How you figure your shit is bigger than mine
These fucked up times and hard core rhymes
Got you throwing up gang signs
And claiming coasts or shades of color
Which shameless boasts of emotionless lovers
That gaze upon the ice that clutter the pendant
Of That religion you do not follow
Your faith has evaporated and made your soul hollow
Childhood dreams turn pharmaceutical schemes got
    you fucking with triple beams

def poetry jam on broadway

Cap peeling robbing and stealing
For a piece of this fucked up
American pie ass nigga
Ready to die ass nigga
Fly ass nigga
Sit you in a cell you probably cry ass nigga
How the fuck you figure your shit is bigger
Than mine
I see you diamond blinking
Cuban Linking and full length minking
All strung out on disillusional thinking
And as the government subsidizes
These laboratory high rises
With new chemical surprises
You continue to hide your true self
Behind movie gangsta' disguises
Oblivious to what life's true prize is
Equating stupidity with the length you
Think your dick size is
The truth in your eyes is
Falsify, fabricated while you sit
And wait for your fate to be debated
By juries and judges who've held
Over four hundred and fifty years
Worth of grudges
Nigga get back, sit back and rediscover
How to be an honest father
Loyal lover
Righteous brother
And not just another
Motherfucking nigga.

# i write
# AMERICA

*written by* **The Company**

**suheir**    I write America a Dear John letter
I'm not leaving but things have to
get better
Learn to pronounce my name correctly
I am taxpayer
and brick layer
These poems are us
Our history,
you have no choice but to recognize
me and mine
for the fire next time,
I rewrite America.

**poetri**    I write America for the people just like me,
too busy blamin' instead of claiming
that America is the best place to be.
This is my family
Yea, my kin folk have problems and issues
like every family does
but I'm going to make my difference right
here
for us
I write America

**mayda**    I dream America for the day I won't have
to hyphenate my identity
For the day everyone will be tri-lingual
For the day I won't be asked where I'm
really from or complimented on how
well I speak English

For the day the American dream includes me
I write America

**staceyann**  I write America for the
not-so-funny-face
of Will and Grace
That dear old, queer old USA
Langston Hughes, Zora Neale Hurston,
James Baldwin...
For the voices who broke the silence
I write America.

**lemon**  I will always write America for the poor people
And I'm not trying to tell you how to live
but vanity will kill you so will MTV Cribs
For the poor people, I write America.

**steve**  I write America
love notes in my protest poems
Because this is my home
Because between the shining seas
and redwood forests
I am one voice in a chorus
composing ourselves from wounded knees
We write America
because even when it's not
we assume that it's free
We write America.

**black ice**  I would write America
but I'm too suspicious
I know
the powers that be
are vicious
and they wouldn't
have a problem

sacrificing the lives
of twenty five hundred people
at the bottom of Manhattan
in order
to boost their economy.
See, they've been sacrificing the lives
of the youth around my way
to fill their filthy pockets
since I can remember
So instead
I just watch America.

**beau**   I have to write America
because no one else will do it for me
Chinatown is America,
Bruce Lee is America
my mother is America.
My people
you should never have to accept less
never view yourselves as other
and never have to
fear internment again
I am America.

**georgia me**   I CHANGE AMERICA…by living life to the fullest
Fight those who try to pull shit and always
resist the unjust system
I serve only Him or She, so
I write to free my brothers and sisters
no matter what the color.
Speak only the truth
so the blind can see
WE MUST MAKE AMERICA
A TRUE DEMOCRACY.

*End of Show.*

beau **SIA**

black **ICE**

georgia **ME**

**LEMON**

mayda **DEL VALLE**

**POETRI**

staceyann **CHIN**

steve **COLMAN**

suheir **HAMMAD**

dj tendaji **LATHAN**

beau SIA

"I want all poems to be about me!" he spits from the stage of the Longacre Theatre on New York's Broadway. A far cry from the thoughtful, unassuming young man that is Beau Sia.

Growing up in Oklahoma City, he was the lone Asian kid among a sea of faces that did not look like his own. As typical of many people who grow up outside of their culture of origin, Beau wanted to be something more than just **"the Asian kid."** But comments from his non-Asian friends like, "you don't even *act* Asian," stung just the same, causing him to question his concept of the Asian identity; a theme that would later surface in his writing.

Beau began to write poetry for the same reasons plenty of teenage boys do things; to impress a girl. And although he didn't get the girl, he got writing. In fact he got it so much that after graduating high school, he decided that he was going to go to New York to perfect his craft—even if he had to extort his parents to do it. They, being parents, were fully against his going to school for something they saw little future in. He said, "I told you 'I won't go to college at all if I can't go for writing!'" He won the standoff and enrolled in New York University's dramatic writing program. Encouraged by professors who saw real talent in him, his "anger and angst" developed into tangible themes, which form the core of his written expression to this day: Love and the lack thereof; his Asianness; America's exclusion of people of color who make the **"melting pot"** what it is.

These, along with his personal peeves and quirks, comprise the body of his spoken word language. It is this language that brought him to countless poetry slams and an appearance in the movie *Slam*, two shots at HBO's *Def Poetry,* and finally to the Broadway stage. His parents had been to the play several times and couldn't be prouder. Vindicated that the path he pushed for was the right one, Beau is more than satisfied his dreams are being met in more ways than even he imagined.

"Broadway was definitely the bomb, but it was hard to do the same material every night. It's hard to get back to the same emotional place every time." But the play has matured him as an artist and performer. "I never had to collaborate on what I wrote with other poets before. It was very hard." That collaboration has helped his personal growth also. "I've grown up since Broadway. I'm only twenty-six but having to be on time and responsible to other people had a very positive effect on me. I've never had a real job before, and this was definitely a real job."

"The *Def Poetry* project has moved the spoken word into the forefront of the nation's consciousness," Beau says, reflecting on the larger meaning of the show. But he feels it has had mixed effects on today's youth. "Plenty of these kids doing spoken word now are treated like rock stars. They are missing the point of poetry as self-expression," he quips sardonically. "But it has also brought a lot of kids together around the things affecting their world, who might not have even spoken to each other."

Beau has plans beyond Broadway. He's hoping that one result of the exposure afforded him by the show is a multibook deal. "At the end of the day, I'm just a writer," he says modestly. As Beau says in one of his pieces, "You're not shutting me up until the egg roll is recognized as an American food!"

# CHOICES

**beau sia**

maybe you'll forget this poem when you wake up
tomorrow.

maybe we'll be at war when this airs.

maybe more will come from this.

maybe poets will become famous.

maybe they'll allow sudden stardom to warp their reality.

maybe I'll help this.

maybe I'll get caught up.

maybe I'll start writing with the consumer in mind.

maybe Viacom will tell the world that this is poetry.

maybe my poems will be everywhere.

maybe women will fuck me because of my image.

maybe I'll confuse sex with power.
maybe I'll confuse power with love.
maybe emma will leave me.

maybe I'll lie to myself more.

maybe I'll get lazy.

maybe I'll get assistants.
    I mean, yes men.

maybe I'll assume I can do anything.

maybe I'll assume I can do anything
    Without having to commit to the work.

my assistants will agree.

maybe I'll become a poet/novelist/actor/screenwriter/
    rockstar/rap icon.

all of the novelists, actors, screenwriters, rock stars, and
    rap icons will despise me.

it won't matter.
the name beau sia
will let me do whatever I want.

maybe my management will make my choices for me.

maybe I won't even be aware of any of this.

maybe I'll stop questioning.

I'll say to myself,
"you're great.  You're rich.  You're loved.  Your fans want
    to be you.  You're brilliant.  But keep writing what
    works."

maybe I get afraid.

maybe I don't want to lose my success.

maybe I stop writing.

maybe I'll live through previous accomplishments.

maybe I forget parts of me.

maybe I forget
       that I was 17, I lived in Oklahoma,
       and I needed to write.

to constantly process my teen angst world.

that high school me who wanted tv appearances and
   financial success,
but knew that
the only thing I would ever own
would be my writing.

and maybe I'll never lose that hunger to explore.
   Experiment.  Create.

but I'm afraid.
I'm getting more famous everyday.

don't get me wrong.
I love these blessings.

but I don't want to forget the gift that got me here.

so I want to tell you
that if I fall.

if trl and my agent consume me.

maybe you'll have this last me before the sitcom life.

maybe you'll ask if your choices
will bring you to this place.

maybe you'll wake up tomorrow
and remember
that before all of this,

we were just poets.

# IF I WAS
## YOUR BEST FRIEND

**beau sia**

I would tell you

How bad

Your acting is

To your face.

# UNICORN
## dream

**beau sia**

I've held you in front of blinking manatees,
Tucked moonlight
Into secret places for you,
And together
We've seen some of the lamest
Teen comedies
Hollywood has to offer.

But you failed to see
The magic in that.

Or rather,
Failed to need
Nurturing simple gifts
The way I did.

The past had you
Looking around corners
We hadn't gotten to yet.

The anxiety building
Like
The gas accidentally left on
In the kitchen.

And my mouth a match,
Where even the word 'love,'
Caused brutal explosions.

You always found
Things to fill your hands with
In public,
To insist separation.

I don't know how many shirts of mine
I've stopped wearing
Because you loved taking them off,

But it is going on 15 months since
We shared a smoothie,
      A couch,
      A sunburn,

And it is 15 months into
Never having resolved this time
Together in our lives.

I'd email you to say wassup
And salvage any warmth between us
I could,

But this not-so-often-anymore ache
Is better, at least,
Than feeling lost in a conversation
With someone
I once considered home.

"We are the inherent carriers of the words of the earth. See, we've been destined to do this shit since birth . . ." When Lamar "Black Ice" Manson wrote this, he thought it was just a poem. Something to spit out that sounded fly. Fast-forward a few years and Black Ice would be doing a stand-in at a program at Martin Luther King high school in Harlem, for a no-show Ja Rule. High school kids tend to get a bit salty when they expect a hip-hop mega star and get a relatively unknown poet. But Black Ice hit them upside the head. After he was done, kids were coming up to him with tears in their eyes, telling him how much he touched them; how powerful and real his words were. "It was the first time I really knew that this poetry shit was something I was supposed to do. I mean my words really reached those kids."

The Philadelphia streets grew his POTENT POETRY. Lamar didn't grow up soft. His father was a mixed bag of signals. On the one hand, he was an ardent and outspoken defender of African-American civil rights, and on the other, he was a crafty street hustler who sold drugs and existed outside of the law. He never steered young Lamar away from street life, his advice being that aspects of the hustler's game were better left alone until he got some more age under his belt. It's no wonder that Lamar was selling drugs by the tender age of thirteen, something that was not so uncommon in his "hood" at the time. However, before he started hustling, Lamar developed a talent and love for art. In the second grade, he was drawing comics of figures he appropriated from Heavy Metal magazine and selling his finished product to his classmates. The twist he put on his figures was that they were all engaged in various sex acts. Later, graffiti was his portal into the world of hip-hop. He then moved to beat boxing and by sixteen, had his own group, the Bandits. He proudly exclaims, "We once opened for Stetsasonic," the popular hip-hop act. He was a local shining star, both as a hustler and a fledgling hip-hopper. "I grew up slinging coke and rapping, but finally, I settled down and became a barber and coke dealer. I was still a barber up until about a year ago." Black Ice now spends most of his time performing and has been on the stage with a number of hot mainstream rap and R&B acts, including his old friend from Philly, recording star Jill Scott. "Writing and performing releases me from the prison of self. I get air from writing. When I decided to leave the street game my words and my life began to flourish."

Broadway was a hard routine for an ex-hustler to crack, but "Ice" never missed a show; a testimony to how much he's turned himself into the messenger of the earth he was destined to be. "Every night I had to re-invent those poems because there is someone out in that audience that needs to hear what I'm about to spit."

When Black Ice is off stage, he is building. First, his band, Anti-Nigger Machine, which backed him up on his new DVD, soon to be released by Def Jam Records. And secondly, an artist management company called Step Lightly Artist Development, that he's formed with his homeboy, Dion "Q" Turner. While Black Ice has elevated himself above street hustler, he did not abandoned the streets for the lights of Broadway. He's still keeping it real.

# THE SHORT END
# OF THE STICK

**Black Ice**

The little guy
watched as his
mother and
father
scurried to gather
what they could
carry in their arms...
Harms way was coming
in the
name of
liberation.
The little girl watched
her mother
and father
hug and
kiss and
cry as
he set off to
defend a questionable
declaration.
She stood in front
of the t.v.
at attention
with her hand
in military salutation
with an innocent look of pride
on her face
as the first bombs
were deployed.
He stood
barefoot on the sandy hills
outside his town
with tears in his eyes
watching his
home destroyed...
in the name
of
liberation.

black ice

121

# THE WORDS

**Black Ice**

spokenword
is poetry intertwined
in a harmonious
twister
dedicated to the transmission
of conscious word
out to
the listener
them being
the drinker
while
we speak the drink
sliding smoothly
through your
soul
causin' your 3rd eye
to blink
makin' you think
and blink
deeper and deeper
into
mental glasses of
flavor
dynamically expressed through
ascetic behavior
the words??
the words come from
within in us
they began in us

repeating
'cause that ancestral african
drum be in us
constantly beating
inspiring us
to poetically
speak on the now
and here
but
speak that same shit our
people speak
so understand us
loud and clear.
oh, proud with cheer we are
if we come off
and ya'll are all
clapping and whistling.
but
we'd be pissed to the joint
if ya'll missed the point
cause ya'll wasn't listening.
see the words,
the words be like food
used to stimulate
the brain.
lettin' my brothers and sisters
know
they don't have to immulate
to maintain.
colonial culture
has left a horrible
stain
got us living in vain
tryin to ignore

the internal pain
that we see
and hear
in momma's eyes
and
babies cries
instead
we live out true lies
through man made get highs
and unwed young wet thighs.
african kings and queens
cloaked in european disguise
seems we've taken our eyes
off the prize.
but the words i convey
don't contain sex
guns or violence
if i can't say something positive
the alternative
is
silence.

# UNTITLED #29384

**Black Ice**

NEVER GET CAUGHT UP
ON LIFE'S
PREVIEWS...
YOU
MIGHT MISS
THE BIG PICTURE.

georgia
ME

"Everyone's a poet," says Tamika Harper, aka Georgia Me. "I'm a spoken word artist," she declares in no uncertain terms. "The difference," she thoughtfully began, "is that I have the ability to take the written word off the page and put my living spirit into the work and make people feel it, you know?" Through her movements, inflection, and temperament—or temper—Georgia Me brings a deeper understanding of what her words say with her presence, standing before you.

"It started when I was eight years old at summer camp, you know, the kind where they bus inner city kids to greener pastures and shit—which we don't have anymore." A drama teacher at that camp got a copy of Nikki Giovanni's *Ego Trippin'* into Tamika's hands and "the word" therein began to transform a little Black girl. *Ego Trippin'* is Giovanni's belligerent, self-affirmation poem that declared Black women to be queens, powerful, resourceful, intelligent, and Black *and* Beautiful. **"I am beautiful, I am a beautiful woman!"** the poem declares. "That was so hard for me at eight years old, being a fat Black girl growin' up in Atlanta . . . in the hood, sayin' that. But for whatever reason, I thought that I could say it, because Nikki said it." For a young girl growing up hearing that being Black was the worst thing in the world, these words had **miraculous healing powers.**

"I didn't really look at myself in a mirror until I was nineteen years old, because I thought I was so ugly." As the darkest child in her family, Tamika was constantly reminded of it in negative ways. "And it wasn't from my Mama or my Grandmamma, who was this big, beautiful, caramel-color, Cherokee-looking . . . ooo, she was just beautiful! She loved my color. It was her sister, who was my color, but would put all this white powder on her face. She never wanted to claim Black, talkin' 'bout 'I'm Cherokee, I'm Cherokeeeeee!' " Giovanni's poem told her that what she was hearing from a self-hating relative, and an anti-Black society at large, wasn't true, and that she and her life as a Black woman had tremendous historical value, just waiting to be tapped.

As her exploration of poetry began, her verbal and cognitive skills grew. She became captain of the debate team, the MC for school plays and other programs, and her confidence also grew. Additionally, she credits teachers "in the hood," who recognized something special in her and helped to hone her talents. "I can't really talk about other people and their experiences with bad teachers who don't encourage kids and can't teach," she says, "because I didn't have any bad teachers. All of mine pushed me."

She doesn't remember when she first started writing poetry, but once she did, she wrote about everything: poems to cheer on the high school football team; poems to talk her friends in to and out of stuff, like enlisting in the service; poems about how she felt about boys (of course). And then there was her breakthrough poem, "Sista to Sista," which she wrote in March of 1998, after a particularly poignant realization about something that many young women face at one time or another. One night during one of her early transitional phases, between "Ghetto Princess" and what might be called a more natural style, she and a friend went to see a Goodie Mob concert, . . . "at Club 559 . . . in the hood, where all the gangsters, all the killers, all the drug dealers be," dressed in "Afrocentric" gear, complete with headwraps. To their absolute amazement, she and her friend received the utmost respect from the "players and hustlers," while her scantily clad counterparts received both physical and verbal abuse from the same guys that were bumping into Tamika and saying, "excuse me sista." "Meanwhile there's this one girl right in front of us whose pussy's getting grabbed," Tamika says, relishing the irony. "You could see she really don't like it, but she's missing three teeth, so I guess she feels like this is what she got to deal with." Now why'd she have to put it like that? But the insights keep coming. "You can get people, and they're beautiful, but they'll have one flaw and they'll let that be enough to allow themselves to be used."

Georgia says she liked the collaboration with the other poets in the Broadway production. "I've always worked with other people and it's not like anyone told me what to write. We wrote what we felt separately and then we brought it together. This poets' bond helped us to become better people." Georgia found she learned an incredible amount from the other poets, like "learning how not to be so cheap with myself." She let some of the other cast members convince her to splurge on a fly pair of Gucci glasses that cost $200. "These things were so pretty on me, I had 'em worked into the show!" But then she lost 'em. "So I am back to five-dollar sunglasses, but I bought five pairs."

"Being on Broadway was dope, I give thanks to Mr. Simmons and Mr. Lathan for putting me in the show." She didn't call her producers Russell and Stan. "Naw, I like to keep things a little more formal; I got to show some respect for the Niggods."

The only complaint Tamika had about being on the road is missing her two-year-old son, Wisdom Inshallah, the latter of which translates into "be the will of God," a name she got from a Goodie Mob track. "I love the Goodie Mob. Their music means everything to me." As for her son, Tamika wants to continue to raise a strong Black man and believes that the mind-expanding experiences she's had on the road and with the other cast members has contributed to that goal. Beyond her own child, Georgia Me also hopes that her poetry can be inspirational to some other kids, like Nikki's was for her, when she was just a little Black girl in Atlanta, beginning to figure it all out.

# and YOU wonder

## Tamika

You ever see a child and they
look eleven but are actually only seven
developed physically beyond their years
or extremely obese kids who are taunted with jeers
or babies with rotten teeth
from eating way too many sweets
You ever wonder why little girls look like little women or
    just look old
why our children stay sick their bodies can't fight a cold
Our children everyday eat sugar puff chocolate
    marshmallow
frosted flakes never wheaties
And ya wonder why the number one killer among African
    American is diabetes
58,000 children in the Atlanta at lunch choose between
    french fries & green beans
that's why they stay slow & fat not lean and mean
craving for sweets & fat like a fiend
Olympic gold is an unbelievable dream
12 years old and can't run half a block
watching tv or playing video games like a big rock
no exercise just waisting time watching the clock
Do the mother's really care or just to busy to notice
Their own unhealthy, fat, lazy children who are too hyped
    on sugar to focus
Bottom line unhealthy children become unhealthy adults
which increases their chances to die
Fatal epidemics, decreasing life expectancy and you
    wonder why

# we are such STUFF THAT dreams are made of

**Tamika**

I am in existence because of dreams
just the thought created me
I am from He or She whatever you know God to be
but you can allow destruction to reign with a simple refrain
    of
it's not my problem You shun instruction, on healing pain
but no help on how to solve em
In the minds of many is a utopia of peace
with knowledge and understanding
In our world are lost soldiers at war with rank
and no commanding fallen prey to the demanding day to
    day
grinding all night to make that pay
Walking blind in day light can't find a way
No regard for human life recognized
All have strayed Strayed away from love
The love of the mother with no assistance
but she stays persistant she has children to feed
she consistant cuz in the distance she sees her fruit
    succeed.
The faith of the man who said I will fly, the faith of people
    who made
Hitler cry the faith of kings who said I'll try the faith of a
    poet
Who knows subjection will die

LEMON

**Lemon ain't grow up easy.** The half Puerto Rican kid from Sunset Park, Brooklyn, grew up an outlaw and describes his parents as outlaws too. Both parents belonged to a gang called the F.M.Ds ("Floor Master Dancers" or "Filthy Mad Dogs," depending on the mood of the speaker). Both were heroin addicts. Both died of AIDS. So his survival skills had to kick in early or he wouldn't be here either.

With both parents dead, Lemon had to fend for himself. He became an armed robber, a drug dealer, and an interstate transporter of narcotics. He took the drug dealing on the road, all the way to Columbus, Ohio, where he was eventually arrested for possession of both drugs and firearms. When he was released, he fled back to New York, where he wound up in jail for robbery. Jail might have been a lucky break for Lemon, because it was in the infamous Rikers Island he found his **love of reading and poetry**. With nothing but time on his hands, Lemon looked for positive role models in the jail-house poets he read and met while doing his bid. He began writing the "Why Me" series, detailing his trials and tribulations behind bars. After eighteen months, Lemon was released again, essentially homeless and broke. Fate took him to the poetry slam in Williamsburg, Brooklyn, where he persuaded fellow cast member Suheir Hammad to let him read. It was one of those life-changing episodes for young Lemon. The audience went bananas. Nobody had heard such a raw, **urban voice** before.

lemon

Jail and redemption were quite different themes from the more esoteric stuff floating around the NYC poetry scene in the mid nineties. His work was so moving that an executive of El Puente, the community-based social action organization, offered him a job.

A year later, a warrant from Ohio for his arrest had caught up to him. El Puente organized "Lemon Aid," an initiative to ensure the reformed poet got a fair shake in Columbus. He did.

Later, a Bronx-based performance group called the Universes recruited Lemon and he began learning his stage chops. Poet Reg E. Gaines, who was then working on *Bring in Da Noise, Bring in Da Funk* with Savion Glover, befriended him. Reg E. became a mentor and an inspiration from whom Lemon continued to learn. But neither his famous new friends nor the newly found fame of his own has caused Lemon to forget those who'd had faith in him because "Loyalty is important to me," he says. He still works with the Universes and in 2001, they wrote, produced, and starred in an award-winning play called *Slanguage*. Lemon was an essential element in that effort. "My stuff is profound," he brags a little. "I'm speaking for the poor peoples."

His highly developed sense of a work ethic doesn't leave time for the bullshit. At the time of this interview, he was busy writing *The Notorious B.I.G Musical*, a work about the life of fallen rap icon Biggie Smalls. As talented as he is as a writer and performer, Lemon insists that at his core he is essentially "just a poet." But he's so much more that that. He has continued to use "Lemon Aid" to promote his own work with kids in the various correctional facilities he visits in and around New York State.

Lemon is like "Shine the Stoker," in his poem "The Titanic." He's not about to let nothing or no one break his stroke.

# AALIYAH

Lemon

Since you was born
you must've been told every
	other day
that you were the next Marvin
	Gaye
that you sang my funny
	valentine
just like Billie Holiday
and every pimp walked by with
	a business card
trying to put you on
but you kept your business
	personal
so your family took you on
giving you your first taste of
	stardom
remember how it hurt
yet you smiled even though you
	lost
to a soulless child on star
	search
you went home that night
knowing everything was good
your mamma said from than on
you wouldn't be singing for Ed
	McMahon
you would be singing for your
	hood
you walked in shadow grew up
	shy
when they called you baby girl
you wanted the world to love
	you for your songs
before they loved your baby
	brown pearls
just a shortie
honey but you showed the
	players you don't play
that's rare nowadays it takes
	most women a lifetime
to finally act that way
this is not my imagination
what im saying I mean is true
if I was god and I had all the
	stars
I would take you with me too
I know your family still mourns
I know you fans still cry
But they must know that you a
	real star
And real stars belong to the
	sky

# LEMON'S HAIKUS

**Lemon**

I.

Now when a bitch comes
Around and fucks up your flow
Best let that hoe go!

II.

There sure aint nothing
Holy bout them holidays
Livin in the hood

III.

The worst thing about
Doing a bid in prison
Is coming back home

IV.

Talent is gods gift
To you what you do with it
Is your gift to god

mayda
DEL VALLE

Precious few people realize a life-long dream, as did Mayda Del Valle. As a little girl, she saw Rita Moreno perform at the Longacre Theatre. She knew immediately that she wanted to be on that stage too. Years later, on that same stage, Mayda gets thunderous applause from an audience on opening night after performing her poem "Descendancy."

This Puerto Rican woman from the Windy City (Chicago), stands up tall on that stage—**all five feet one inch of her** —and gives homage to the ancestors that brought her this far. "I can't deny the fact that Yoruba songs lay in the lines of my mother's palms/as offerin' up psalms . . ."

"I ain't gonna front," she says. "I've always wanted to be a star. Even as far back as six years old, when I'd make up skits and perform them for my family." She started writing poetry at fourteen and by sixteen, she was working and performing at the Gould complex in Chicago. In high school, one particular teacher, Mrs. Kelly, became her mentor and directed her energies into writing short stories and essays. She joined the school's theater club and starred in countless after-school productions. Mayda pushed herself and in between the writing and performing, she began taking Puerto Rican folk dance classes. It was here that she began to learn of her **"Afro-Boricua ancestry."** Her instructor made sure she understood the roots of her culture and how African influences informed the dance, song, and religion of the Puerto Rican people.

mayda del valle

After high school, Mayda attended Williams College in Massachusetts where she became part of a small but vocal "minority" student population. Looking for a valid medium to express herself, she tried sculpture for a few years but was constantly being drawn back to the performing arts. She took video classes, taping herself performing her poetry. She began to look to other poets for inspiration, identifying with the leading poets of the late 1990s: Saul Williams, muMs, Jessica Care Moore, and felt a bond with the revolutionary themes laced through their works.

In her senior year, she was criticicized by the other students for wanting to perform her work in Spanish. This only heightened a growing estrangement from the mainstream. A trip to South Africa opened her eyes to the depth of poverty and the resilience of the human spirit as embodied by African people. These themes are all threaded throughout her work. It was that level of spirit and understanding that landed her on the Longacre's stage.

The collaboration with Lemon on the Tito Puente piece was hard for Mayda, but also very rewarding. The director had to step in several times to help the two poets achieve the wonderfully balanced piece that is presented during the show.

Actor/performance artist John Leguizamo is providing the road map for the type of career Mayda wants to achieve. She can clearly see being the star of her own one-woman show on the Great White Way. With Mayda stepping out on the stage, the Great White Way just got a little darker. As Rita Moreno had before her, Mayda intends to help fill the void of positive role models for young people of color.

# ACADEMIA
## leaves my tongue
## HEAVY

**Mayda Del Valle**

academia leaves my tongue heavy
filling my mouth with acidic saliva
that
burns away all traces of intellectual languages
and leaves me slurring through my native tongue
im caught in the
middle
of two places
negotiating where im from
with where i am
trying to mix my urban tongue
with the bookish knowledge ive acquired

i retreat to dark spaces
in the back of my throat
where the guttural sounds are primitive and unformed
where the thought
and the sound
meet
to form the word

# SEDUCE me

**Mayda Del Valle**

seduce me
write me a poem
tell me about the scent of musk at the nape of my neck
that you dream of spending sultry summer days between
    my breasts
that if you could taste me
it would be mangoes and tropical breezes on your tongue
keeping you up at 2am
for weeks
staring at black ceilings
legs entwined in sheets
wiping your brow
wondering when the next will be
seduce me
write me a poem
drop those weak pick up lines
and overwhelm me with quotes from Nerudas 100 love
    sonnets
tell me i walk in beauty like the night
trace the lines in the palm of my left hand
decipher
then read and whisper their meaning
to me
tell me my life line crosses your destiny
imprint your words on me like overnight scratchmarks
leave butterflies in my stomach
with honeysuckle syllables
that remind me of first kisses
and holding hands at recess

seduce me
write me a poem
that prays my name
and preaches our passion
chant a litany of our lovemaking to come
under your breath
with the faith of whithered hands holding rosaries in
    cathedrals
until images of us entwined in each other
burn themselves inside our minds
like incense at mass
seduce me
write me a poem
with your eyes
lock glances for a moment
across a crowded room
soft smirk on full lips
and a slow deliberate blink followed by a flutter of
    eyelashes
that's says
damn I wish...
seduce me
write me a poem
with your body
approach me with the certainty of the tide
move to me without doubt or question
make me your origin
and your destination
let music be the catalyst that lets our bodies meet
spin me in and out of conga rhythms
lead me into a Coltrane wail
grind me into the bass-line
of *between the sheets...*
then pull me close enough

to feel our hearts beat together
when we dance
seduce me
write me a poem
that
that speaks of our timelessness
remind me it was you I loved in a past life
on some faraway continent
tell me i carry you in my genes
that i can't forget you if i tried
that our memories are engraved into eternity
that time is just a theory to us
seduce me
write me a poem
that needs no words
compose a silent sonnet on soft bare skin
where your caress on exposed back
speaks the syllable i need to hear you
a poem
where melding bodies become
the book
where shallow breathing becomes prose
where
you
seduce me
and
inspire me to write you the poem
that shows you how to love me

# tongue TACTICS

**Mayda Del Valle**

i remember
someone once said
to me
ugh
Puertoricans and Dominicans sound
sooo uneducated when they speak Spanish
cutting off all those letters
it's so lazy
at least even the poorest most uneducated Mexican
will speak to you in "proper" Spanish

and I had nothing to reply with
anger ate the words out my mouth
and I swallowed back the acidic comeback which
   consisted of something like
pue vete p'al carajo cabron!
but
your
verses I subvert
my comebacks come quicker now
mouth opens wide with retorts
in defense of the inflections in my accent
in defense of the articulations of my cultural enunciations
in other words
i'm defending sounding like a damn Puerto Rican

and I got
words doing Mary Lou Retton type flips off my tongue
slurring syllables

warring accents
authenticity goes to shit
Spanglish slips off my lips
and
i'm speaking in tongues
blending proper
with street
talk
everyday
meets academic
bastardizing one language
creating new ones
illegitimate unions between
past and present
give birth to shaky speech structures
makes my expression easier
leaves language purists scratching at their ears

ain't
gonna
get
grammatics
correct
i'm overcome by urban street tinged tongue tactics
this         city slicker demeanor ain't acted
out
i'm taking out all traces of proper English
punctuation's only bein' used to give feeling
no pauses
caesuras non-existent
this vocal pattern is just now bein' enacted
independent of margins that hold my syllables
in check
i'm declaring a state of language revolution

all the words in our vocabulary have declared a universal
    strike
announcing that we have been practicing unfair talking
    laws and not paying them for their
hard labor
threatening to leave our civilization speechless

all accent marks are attending an emphasis convention at
    Webtser's place
the vowels are demanding to be worth at least $2000 on
    the wheel of fortune
Shakespeare's sonnets      are making record deals with
    Puffy to be sung in rap form

dictionaries are on Prozac suffering from an acute identity
    crisis
claiming they can no longer provide all the meanings to
    words in our lives
they now want to tell stories
and
thesaurus's are translating into ebon-glish-espan-chino-
    con-zulu-jammin'-german-parlez-yo-frances-con-portuges-
    con-patois-mon-creole-combining-creating
sounds that is music to my ears
y pue' pentejo a mi no me importa si tu cree que mi
    espanol is not as good as yours !!!


i'm crossing borders
abriendo puertas
tongue waggin'
clickin' off the roof of my mouth
rolling ere's

comiendo ese's
yo tengo el toque de tito's
timbalero
kimbara kimbara kimba kim bam bam
kimbara kimbara kimba kim bam bam
writhing on my lips
i'm riding waves of
language deconstruction

wear ur hardhats
little chicken head !!!!
coz the alphabet is falling from the sky !!!

im daring to deliver dialects
not commercially created
and destroy your nit-wit imbecilic notions
of what language I should speak

ain't gonna get gramatics correct
i never suffer
from a lack of lovely
luscious
lingual
lullaby-like
syllables flowing off these lips

don't give a damn if it's grammatically correct
don't give a shit if you think it's incorrect
i never lack the abiliti to come correct

so get hip to this style papiiiii !!!!!

'cause  i dare you to come over and
write a 15 page analytical essay due by Tuesday at four in

    my mailbox
on any subject of your choosing
that moves the crowd
like WHOA!

and read it on a mic
and read it on a mic

and read it in your uptight
educated sounding proper tongue

'cause
i'll still be here
with these tongue tactics
never getting gramatics correct
and still making these folks go

like whoa.

# "I wasn't even joking man. I was dead serious when

I wrote that. I got on stage and started doing my thing, and everybody fell out laughing. I was pissed and confused. I didn't see a damn thing funny at the time." It's hard to imagine that the man known as Poetri wasn't trying to be comical when he wrote, "My money's been acting funny lately/and all I ever did was love her," but the empathic irony of his words hits deep chords within all of us. I've heard it a dozen times or more and still laugh every time. "I wrote that poem when I WAS DEAD BROKE and couldn't see where my next dollar was coming from. I really was feeling that my money had been acting funny lately."

And although he is also the host of one of the largest poetry venues in the nation, Da Poetry Lounge, he says he never saw the poetry thing coming. Poetri says he began using poetry as a 100 percent release because "all I wanted to do was act."

The product of a strong middle-class background, Poetri's creative bent was nurtured and encouraged by his family. His brother is a professional writer and his sister is an actor/director. His own career has been as DIVERSE as the feelings he expresses on stage. He's written a few screenplays; acted in commercials; done voice-overs; radio broadcasts, and the list goes on. *Def Poetry* director Stan Lathan caught him doing his act and invited him to audition for the HBO show. Apparently grooming himself for fame all along, the hop from the television show to the Broadway stage was short.

poetri

Having spent most of his creative career working alone, it took some adjusting to work comfortably with other poets. Whatever the struggle behind the scenes to do so, his collaborations appear effortless on stage. "Metaphors," by Poetri and Steve Colman, is collaboration at its zenith. The words and timing flow to perfection. Poetri's collaborative efforts off stage are of equal importance to him. Together with his sister, he has worked on eight consecutive annual Peace Days in Los Angeles County. It's an event that brings kids together from all ethnic and economic strata for a day of music, poetry, dialogue, and fun. The hope is that events like this will promote better inter-ethnic understanding and future alliances and cooperation between people of diverse backgrounds.

Poetri loves performing spoken word, but is eager to use his talents for dramatic acting. He already acknowledges, in one of the pieces he performs in the show, that he spends some time acting like he's Michael Jackson. At least he says he does.

# URGES

Poetri

I have the urge to jump over the counter at McDonalds
    and
make my own Chicken McNuggets.
Cause I'm tired of telling them that I want them fresh and
I'll wait the five minutes and
they still give me some hot, nasty, microwave, re-cooked
    ones!

I have the right mind to slap the lady that tells me,
"They are fresh." No, they're aren't!
Don't you ever have the urge to just punch people?
Sometimes for no reason, but especially when they do or
    say something
stupid.
Too bad, I think sometimes, that my nice body doesn't
    react to my mind's
first reactions.

Cause whenever I walk into a library,
I have the urge to start yelling.
Then I wanna punch the first person that tells me,
    "Shhhh, this is a
library."
Like I don't know!
I have this cruel urge to slap anyone that says libary. It's
    a library!

I have this weird urge to walk into Supercuts and demand
    a haircut,
even though I know they don't cut black folk hair.

My urges are mean. They're like my evil twin.
Like I have the urge to go grab that girl's booty right there.
Everyone who knows me, knows I would never do that,
    though.
I mean, of course, unless she asked me.
I have the drive to go rob a bank on broke days
or go steal some money out of a cash register on some
    days.
Thank God I would never actually do that.
Yet, am I criminal for thinking criminal thoughts?
A hoe for thinking hoe thoughts?

I have the urge to go stand on the 405 freeway and
hold my hand up and see how many cars I can get to stop.
I have the urge to get hit by one of those cars
to see who would come to my funeral.
Just cause I have the desire to find out who really loves
    me...do you?

Am I the only one? Do other people think about doing
    things that they would
never do?
Am I the only one that says to myself...What if?
What if I did this? What if I did that?
What if I stood in the middle of the Beverly Center buck
    naked?

Okay, maybe you don't think that and
maybe that was just a little too much information,
but you know what am I saying.
What if we all acted out our urges?

I'd be dead or in jail, right now, or in insane asylum with
    Unsane.
Trying to refrain from thinking that I'm on the Midnight
    train to Georgia,
with Glady's Knight and one Pip, with a busted lip, and a
    messed up hip,
still talking 'bout that trip on the Midnight, man, we done
    flipped it if we
acted out our impulses.

I have the urge to keep rhyming like that.
I have the urge to become a cop so that I can arrest other
    cops.
I have the itch to tell the IRS that they can keep calling
    and sending mail,
but
I'm not gonna pay them the money I owe until I get the
    money.
I have the longing to tell telemarketers to kiss my ass!
I have the urge to splurge, no work, just play all day,
walk around cussing all day, having sex all day,
but I can't do that. I won't do that.
I'm a full fledge Christian. At least I try to be.
That doesn't mean I don't have urges.
That doesn't mean I don't slip and fall sometimes...okay
    a lot of times.
I have the urge to slap people that criticize us when we do
    fall.
When we fall victims to our urges, our desires, our sins.

Not all my urges are bad and cruel and senseless.
I have some nice urges, some sad urges,
things I need to do urges, things I want to believe urges.

Like I have the urge to believe that things really happen
    like they do in
the movies.
Soon as I step out of the movie theater, reality erases
    that urge.
I have the urge to ask you out.
Shyness always blocks that one.
The urge to cry in public,
my manhood bullies that away.
The urge to sing...
Yolanda Adams or Kurt Carr and the Kurt Carr singers.
I usually act on this urge and
don't let me put Michael Jackson in the walkman.

Urges are a funny thing. Can you judge a man by his
    urges?
If so, then I am a pretty weird guy, leading a double life.
But, I don't think so, urges are what they are.
Quick thoughts thrown at our brain from whichever angle.
When we decide to act on these urges good or bad, then
    we become them.
Most of us rationalize and think.
And thank GOD that most of us don't act on all of all
    urges.

# END OF STORY

**Poetri**

Some people like to go to the end of a book
to read the conclusion.
I don't understand this.
My mom likes me to tell her the ending of a movie
while she's watching it.
I don't get it.

What's the point
if you already know that she survived the car crash
and got psychic powers from the concussion blast,
and saved her ex-husband from the killer, at last.
Why am I going to still pay my ten dollars?

You're taking the Wind out of the gone.
the Sixth out of the Sense,
the color out of the Purple,
and the Purple out of the Rain.

The Soul out of the Game.

You're missing out on the drama.
Yet, even when I tell my mama that
she still jumps and closes her eyes at all the right parts.
Deep down in her heart she knows the deal from the start.
I know cause I told her the ending.

There are people out there like me,
that don't want to watch the movie

poetri.

or read the book if they know what's gonna happen in
the end.
We don't want to videotape a Lakers' game,
just so you can tell us who won before we get home!
We want to find out ourselves, why... "life's a box of
chocolates,"
We want to cry ourselves when we find to why Malcolm X
got shot.
We want to laugh ourselves when Eddie Murphy says,
"Come on Cleatus. Come on!"

The only ending story I want to read is my own.
I wish I knew how I turned out.
I wish I had the paperback or hardcover in front of me.
It would be a bestseller complete with drama, action,
suspense, and brief nudity.
I'd open it up straight to the last page and see that I made
it.
See how I played it, see all my friends that faded...and
who stayed.

I wish I rented the movie from Blockbuster and was
playing it right now.
I would bypass all the pains of the loneliness,
my cries out to deaf ears,
my hatred of my reflection in glass mirrors.

Fast-forward all the days of my confusion,
I want to know my conclusions.
Skip ahead past the agony of my sinning,
past all the hardship beginning,
I'm looking for my ending.
No need to revisit the streets of my distress,
the tears that I work like a vest.

I don't have a penny right now.

I need to know that I'm gonna survive this!

I want not to worry about who likes me or who doesn't.
I want to know the end of my story.
I'm not concerned with his story,
not even my history, right now!
All I want to know is
am I gonna make it past this hurdle?
Do I come out with my hands up in victory,
praising the Lord and the obstacles he sent to me?!
Am I on my knees, thanking you or begging you still,
am I refusing you or giving all the Glory,
I want to know the end of my story!

If I knew the final episode,
the part where I'm rich, married and old.
The episode where I survived all the things
the devil has thrown at me,
when my character is completely happy.
the time when temptation no longer has a hold of my
    decisions.
The point when there are no more divisions…only God.
The part right before I'm ready to go home.
If I knew all of this
would I still worry about my problems down here?
If I just knew the end and saw my picture crystal clear,
me smiling in heaven with god standing there,
would I still care?

# IF I EVER LOST YOU.

**Poetri**

I had a chilling thought the other day.
If I ever lost you...
It was worse than a nightmare.
The scare woke me up and I wasn't even sleeping.
I thought about how I would feel.
What would I do? You are more than just a better half.
You are a better whole.

If I ever lost you,
I would search every valley low or mountain high to find
    you, again.
First, I would search to find myself,
so that when I was in your presence,
I would have the patience and the nerve
to give you all the attention you deserve.

If I ever lost you,
I would run to the largest cliff that I could find.
The Grand Canyon would be too small
cause I would need to find something bigger, better and
    more beautiful.
Symbolism!
So, as I am jumping off, I can see how awesome you were
    to me.

If I ever lost you,
I would really need to do some serious running!
Cause if my mom found out, not to mention my sister and
    my homies,

they would chase me down and try to beat me down
   before I got to that cliff.
I wouldn't be able to find any beauty in fist and screams
being hurled at me like bad dreams.

They know what you mean to me.
They know what you mean to this world.
It's hard for them to figure out what a girl like you
is doing with a brother like me.
but now that they see that miracles do happen they would surely
beat the mess out of me if I ever lost you.

I would need to run to every movie theater,
every restaurant, every poetry reading, every city,
every home I ever walked into, every single solitary place.
I would search every heart of every person I ever talked to
try and find out where I lost my mind.
Hoping that something or someone could give me a clue.

If I ever lost you,
I would need to run to the funniest comedy club in town,
and pray that a comedian can say something half as funny
as things that you said to me everyday.

I would need to run to every garden
just to see if I could find any confidence growing,
losing you means I lose the seeds of self-assurance
that you planted into my mind every time I was with you.

If I ever lost you,
I would run to the Nuclear bomb plants
trying to find a bomb that was the bomb like you!

I would call 411 and try to get information on how I could
      get you back.
I would sprint to the nearest AT&T or Sprint building
to try to get our communication lines back connected.
I would pay the disconnection fee,
the overdue long distance fee, the hidden charges,
cause if I ever lost you my life would pay the bigger price.

Knowing that you are a Biscuit-head,
I would run to Bisquick to see if they had any info,
run to every oven in the world to see if I could see or
      smell you.

If I ever lost you.

If I ever lost you.
I actually don't know what I would do.
Without you I wouldn't have existence,
cause now
you are all I live for.

# POET ROCK STAR

### Poetri

I've seen a poet walk into a room
and this won't even be at a poetry reading,
I'm just talking a regular room,
like a club or something or maybe even a grocery store,
    doesn't matter
when he walks in, people point and stare in awe,
say things like, "Hey, ain't you...that one poet?"

They may have heard this cat read somewhere or heard
    about him reading
somewhere,
but whatever the reason, he's like semi-celebrity status.
And everybody in the room that knows about spoken word
    knows that he is the
real deal.
They might not know his name, but he still has fame just
    the same,
cause he rocked the mic the other night at the hottest
    poetry club in town
sending the crowd into a frenzy, having everybody want to
    buy his new CD...
which is on sale for 10 dollars, by the way.

Don't let this same poet walk into a poetry reading,
    though.
Oh, man that is a whole new ball game.
See, when he walks into a grocery store, it's different,
you don't expect nothing, you're just happy and amazed to
    see him

shopping at the same store you're shopping at,
but when he walks into a poetry reading...
It's like Miles Davis walking into a jazz joint,
no, maybe this will better clarify what I'm talking about,
it's like Rakim back in the '80s walking into a hip-hop
　　open mic,
or how about George Washington Carver walking into the
　　lab,
you know something is gonna be invented.

The women start to get all hot and giggly in anticipation.
I've always known poets that write poems to get as...
much from a woman as they can get,
nowadays, however, it's taken on new meaning,
now we have bona-fide poetry groupies
that follow you around from show to show,
they gotta know every line to every poem
that you've ever read and if you read that special one,
tonight they might be in your bed.
Wow, ain't it great to be a poet nowadays?

Don't think that this is just a girl thing, either,
nah big, thug looking men, even, be like diggin' on this
　　cat,
they just do it in the cool way that only men can adore
　　someone
cause they know that when this poet takes the stage
he commands attention like a Rock Star.

Poets have become like Rock Stars.
We've become Poet Pop Stars, Poet Divas, Poetry Hip-Hop
　　Stars,

Poetry Hip-Hop Gangsta Rap Stars, Sell-Out Poets,
Keepin' it Real Poets, Afro-Centric Poets, We are the
   World Poets.

And I guess we've always had these, but now the world is
   taking notice.
To be a poet now, is like being a fireman, right after
   September 11,
being a poet is like being an angel and the audience is
   trying to get to
Heaven.
Everybody wants you to save them.
Everybody wants you to say something spiritual to bring
   them out the fire.
They want to be near you, want to hear you speak,
want to hear something that can change their life.

Except, when you become a poet Rock star,
it's different than just being a broke poet like we all once
   were
you ain't always concerned about changing folks life
   anymore.
Just like comedians when they make it big, they ain't as
   funny.
One reason cause they already made the money,
they can't relate as much when their real estate cost
   more than my life
income,
then in come some writers for you to write some funny
   stuff.
I'm waiting for Rock Star poets to have writers write their
   poems
cause they just can't connect anymore

or maybe they just don't have time to write no stupid
    poem,
besides spoken word is about the performance, right?
And Poet Rock Stars sure can perform.

I'm just waiting for the battling.
once poets get signed to major record deals doing videos
with video hoes dancing around a jacuzzi half naked.
Hardly ever heard a woman disgraced in a poem at a
    poetry reading,
she went from Precious African Jewel to a female dog,
because record companies know the true art of selling.

Then the set-up.  The poet conflicts begin.
This poet told that poet off in a poem that's on his latest
    CD.
Hip-hop Gangster poetry will officially arrive,
when poets start proclaiming sets and clicks,
saying stuff like "only poets from the midwest can
    represent".
I tell you, I'm waiting for poets to get murdered over words
    spoken,
when before it was always respect, now they are used to
    put a poet in check

I'm waiting for parents to denounce poetry telling us
it ain't like it used to be when they were growing up
I'm waiting for them to tell me
that they can't tell the ending of someone's poem
from the beginning of another cause all of it sounds the
    same.
Telling me poetry ain't nothing but some trash words
put to music so the little kids can shake their butts, too.

I'm waiting for us to turn into something nothing bigger
    than kids shaking
their butts, too.

I'm waiting.  I pray that I am waiting a long time.
I even pray that I am always waiting and we never get to
    that.
I'm just scared cause I remember when it was about the
    word.
Now I'm not so sure that it is about that anymore.

I'm not sure it's not about how crafty you can say that the
    white man is
keepin' us down.
How many different ways you can describe the female
    genitalia.
Knowing exactly what words to say to make the crowd
    sway
and dig deeper into their wallets to pull out ten dollars
to buy a CD that doesn't even have their favorite poem on
    it.
Do you really feel that way?
What happened to that poet digging deeper into his own
    personal dillemas
and pulling out change to give to the audience.
We used to pay the audience more money than they could
    ever give us
and in return that was our payment,
I remember when we were just honored to do a show.
    Remember that?
Payment was love and appreciation that they wanted you
    to read in the first
place.

That's the cool thing about poetry,
a poet doesn't necessarily write what you want to hear,
but writes what he is feeling at that moment,
and if it is some messed up stuff,
than so be it,
just know that it is real,
heartfelt and wasn't for your approval,
but for my release.

# staceyann CHIN

"Nature grew me up," says Jamaican-born Staceyann Chin. Abandoned by her mother at an early age, Stacey was shuttled between a series of relatives and family friends for most of her childhood. Since her father saw that many of her financial needs were met and was all but absent otherwise, the young Staceyann had to rely on her wits and survival instinct more than on any particular adult.

Smart as a whip, **Stacey excelled in school.** On the power of her intellect, she earned herself a place at a prominent woman's finishing college in Kingston, Jamaica, where she learned the ways of "a proper Jamaican woman." But she was never to become one of that school's prim, marriageable graduates. Stacey was and is a lesbian, a serious taboo in Jamaican culture. So serious, in fact, that Jamaica still has laws on its books making it a crime to even be gay or lesbian. The extreme level of anti-gay and lesbian sentiment in Jamaica is legendary, and Stacey has experienced some of the violence of that bias. She "came out" while attending the University of the West Indies. Instantly, she became persona non grata. Friends abandoned her and strangers taunted her. At one point, several of her male classmates decided that all that she needed to "fix her" was the right type of male sexual attention. They forced her into a bathroom and attempted to gang rape her. Luckily, the vicious assault ended when someone walked in on them.

staceyann chin

After finishing at the university, Stacey wanted only to flee to America. She was unaware of the culture shock that awaited her here. Although ostracized and attacked for her sexual orientation in Jamaica, Stacey had enjoyed "light-skinned privilege" (the intraracial form of racism) afforded her on the island. She quickly discovered that in the U.S. of A., racism against people of color occurs across the board, transcending the shade issue thought to be so important in many Black communities. Although she wanted to shout, "Can't you see how light I am?" the realization resulting from these experiences challenged not only her sense of self, but the way she saw many things, like power relationships and oppression.

These and other circumstances of her youth are quite naturally the food for her pen. Writing became a remedy and an outlet for her anxieties. And after following an attractive woman into the Nuyorican Poets Cafe in the East Village in 1998, Stacey found herself engulfed by the spoken-word experience. She began writing and performing as if born to it. Her first one-woman show with a lesbian theme, performed in Greenwich Village and called *Hands of Fire*, had women throwing their underwear on stage. Just prior to joining the cast of *Def Poetry*, she had completed an equally successful run of her second one-woman show, *Unspeakable Things*.

But poetry aside, Staceyann has become a leading advocate and spokeswoman on the issues that helped to shape, and in some cases distort, her life. Her speaking engagements, ranging in subject matter from child abandonment to gay and lesbian rights, racism and beyond, easily top one hundred per year.

Having to perform the same lines and poems every night was quite a stretch for Staceyann and a bigger challenge than she thought it would be. "I had to dig down very deep night after night to find different motivations for making each performance more powerful than the last."

Her poems are organically political and she writes about the world she experiences; the one of racism, gender, and sexual intolerance and the struggle against other forms of oppression. "I have to write and talk about these issues. It's my contribution to making some lasting change in this fucked up world." The last verse of her poem "Passing" is a belligerent declaration of Staceyann's commitment to that change. "We will still be here, still gay, still black, still human, still surviving in the fact of this blatant bigotry that will one day force us to lace arms so we can all strike back!"

# my grandmother's tongue

**Staceyann Chinn**

She gets shorter every year
her ninetieth birthday bending her into a new century

Now
she has the time to wonder
how the seeds of her womb
have come to such silence

Hearing is hard for her
the twilight taxes the organs of the poor
great-grandmother
she wonders if the children born in exile
look anything like her

American residents
their visits infrequent and few
they bring too many sweets anyway
old people should not partake of such pleasures
dying flesh cannot withstand it

*I don't know the names*
*of the grandchildren in Europe*
*the countries are unpronounceable there*
*the languages spoken with odd pauses*
*and awkward lilts*

*I have buried the umbilical cords*
*that connect me to their future*
*the past lies trapped beneath my tongue*
*my children have taken their children*
*out of my house and I can no longer hear them...*

This is what I imagine she would say
if she had the painted words
prodigal that I am
the daughter of a different land
America has opened its hand
and I am no longer drawn to the place
that birthed me

Wood floors have hardened
to concrete structures stretching
high above my mother's, mother's aspirations

My grandmother has become a ritual of memory
and I am hard pressed to translate
her dialect communicates necessity

Another woman warms my bed

My mother speaks
French phrases in Cologne
her German-Canadian child has never heard
Jamaicans sliding their tongues over the blunt patois
she only dreams of America—home of the faded-blue
    jeans
pale skin and long fingers like mine
oxtails and boiled bananas are foreign to her

staceyann chin

175

Grandma can hardly see anymore
the night falls more quickly for her
familiar words in her mouth reassures her
she mutters Biblical names over and over and over again
impossible to learn new ones
trust in the Lord and be of Good courage
she knows the words of her salvation
foreign names are unnecessary
and how would she say Larah Frederica Hayle Mills-Moller
Diamonique and Sherrel are out of reach

Lisa
might have been possible
but Munich is a lifetime away
and her tenure is close to being over

# my Jamaica

Staceyann Chinn

*My love affair with Jamaica*
*has always been double edged*
two ends of a pimento candle
burning towards a slender middle
the indulgent heat pushing me off-center
    on this island
there has never been safe ground

The flat-cut of Liguanea
contrasts with the fluid shape of indigo mountains
Gordon Town frames the blue-black faces cleaning
dirty windscreens on Hope Road
    the hunger in their eyes eerie at twilight
    the dead breathing wistful flames at night

Rolling across childhood memories
the raspy sound of my brother's breathing
reminds me that I must never rest
the uneven iron bed was never big enough
to hold my dreams - my fears
sweating through the polyester nightgown

Water will always find its own level
my grandmother whispers
    sleep now—before the new day come find you
still looking into yesterday

Jamaica has always been harsh
hard words of rigid correction
connecting with the side of my head

staceyann chin

two fingers of water above the rice
turn down the fire when the pot start boiling
and gal-pickney must learn if wash them under-
clothes

The white uniforms hid the welts on my legs
the blue ties tempered the catholic purity
soft sister-hands encouraged the metal rosary
B+ was never acceptable in Math
you want to sell cigarettes on the roadside?
finish you homework
and come get a piece of cornmeal puddin'

The land has always been lush
coconuts husks split open to the rush of a moody sea

Sunday afternoons on the endless sand
pre-adolescent belly bottoms slit to reveal the red fruit
pulpy sweet but angry in captivity
Jamaica
has always loved me from a place of random beauty
women with wide cassava hips
and full star-apple lips
women with strong hands
reaching beyond their own fears
to give their children courage
teaching them to stand straight-backed
in the absence of fathers who visit
with the smell of white rum in their words

My father has never loved women
with soft hands—my mother will show you the scars
still wrapped around her solid middle
banning her belly tight against visibility

This child will never be silent
I speak now
because my grandmother gave me tongue
I speak now
because Jamaica has always given me
crosses I will have to bear alone
the only compass my mothers needle-sharp pain
shooting proud across my back
marked like a crab
Jamaica has always been able to find me
a thorn among the bloody hibiscus blooms
my Jamaica
has always been
the hardest poem to write

staceyann chin

# Uncle Sam's
# TABLE

Getting used to eating across America can be quite the heart-burning experience. The food is nothing like what can be had from the Jamaican countryside I know, or the uptown eateries in Upper St. Andrew. This here, at Uncle Sam's table is a whole other kettle of fish.

On the way from Kingston to Montego Bay you can stop at Faiths Pen to have a roast corn or a piece of saltfish or a cup of manish water. If you don't want that kind of food, there are a hundred more jerk pork spots that serve a hundred other things to choose from. If you want upscale you can stop at any tourist-type restaurant in Ochi and be fed by soft smiling Jamaicans wearing a multitude of different colored uniforms and no name tags.

Traveling across America, there is MacDonalds, Burger King, Wendys, Fridays, and a few other places that serve the same six things on the menu. I get so tired of French fries and burgers that I know are not burgers anymore. They do so much to the poor cow before they even kill it. Then there is the preserving and the packaging. By the time it gets to that shiny paper in your hand it could very well be a mongrel from one of the backyards in Port Antonio. They have to add beef flavor to it then. Nobody knows what the meat is in that wax paper. The beef taste the same as the cow, as the chicken, as the veggie-meat.

Sometimes, I sit in the cold Taco Bell in Indianapolis and fantasize about the curry chicken my grandmother used to cook. Other times I just bite the frozen chicken nuggets and pretend that it is really a nice piece of fried plantain I eating.

Thank God for the small pockets of the West Indies in Brooklyn. Jamaican food joints all over the place call out to me when I am passing; Golden Crust, Brawta, Buff Patty—In New York, you can get food that is almost as good as the food from Jamdung. Whenever I miss home so bad I only want to play some Bob and talk to other Jamaicans, I pick up my bag and head out to eat at Negril, in Manhattan. The prices are a little steep for the small pocket, but that is New York. And I must tell you 'bout the food! Lawd have mercy! They have everything, red peas soup, callaloo—they even have turn cornmeal on the menu! I don't know what they put in that food, but –hmm hmm, hmm!

And all sorts of people gather at that restaurant, rich, poor, gay and straight. Everybody welcome.

Life so busy here, we hardly get a chance to cook, and for those of us who live far from Flatbush Avenue, or Jamaica, Queens, we can't get the ingredients, so the little we cook is more American than Jamaican. It's a dicey state of affairs—living and eating in this America. But "if you want good, you nose haffi run!"

And while we here in this foreign, but not so foreign country, we running and hoping for good and eating where we can and dreaming of home all the time. If you have the time, cook something Jamaican tonight. If you running against the clock, stop and eat a meal in a place that smell a little like Faith's Pen.
Walk good. Till Next time,

**Staceyann.**
staceyannchin.com

STEVE
COLMAN

"Everybody always spells my last name wrong. There ain't no E in my Colman." Steve has been down with *Def Poetry* from the git go. He traveled with Danny Simmons, Stan Lathan, and a group of other poets to the Aspen Comedy Festival to sell the concept to HBO.

Steve Colman grew up **hip-hop**—about as hip-hop as a white kid living in Englewood, New Jersey could get, I mean. He lived down the block from the Robinsons, founders of Sugar Hill Records; hung out with the little brother of Master G of the Sugar Hill Gang (a kid named Leo); went to an all-Black high school where not only was he in a break dance crew named the Circuit Breakers, he was even voted best MC at his high school. He got family support for his Hip-Hopishness too: his mother was the dance crew's manager. She booked them for their first gig at Steve's father's church. Daddy was a preacher, of all things. His rap group, the Boys of Poise, did small shows all around the area too. Called "Kid Finesse," he and his partner, "MC Style," kicked rhymes like this: "I'm MC Style/he's Kid Finesse/he likes the wings/I like the breast." Only in the early days of hip-hop could a crew get away with lyrics about eating fried chicken.

All this would be great background training. From fried chicken to the witty and powerful political prose he delivers on the Broadway stage, **"I Wanna Hear a Poem"** is Steve's signature piece. He's dead serious when he says, "I wanna hear a poem about revolution/about fists raised high/and hips twisting in a rumble/like a rumba . . ."

Steve didn't think of poetry as his way out . . . or *in* for that matter. He went to college in Minnesota for political history, following behind his twin brother, who, by the way, also rhymed with Steve in another group named the First Family. By 1990, Steve began hanging out back in NYC in places like the Nuyorican Poets Cafe. In fact, he sat in that club for some seven years until he "spit" for the first time in August of '97. Poetry appealed to Steve's sense of the "power of the word." It also appealed to his political sensibilities. He believes that words go farther without the music behind them, obscuring their potency.

His brilliant lyrics about fried chicken not withstanding, poetry has propelled Steve Colman further than rap ever could have. "Being on Broadway is the top and I'm not sure where I can go from there," Steve says after considerable reflection. But one thing he knows is that being on Broadway has "leveled the playing field" with his famous African-American poet/performer, fiancée Sarah Jones. He quickly adds, "Not that there was anything wrong [with her success], but I like being in the same strata as she is." Steve fell in love with Sarah the first time he saw her recite "The Revolution Won't Happen Between These Thighs."

There are only a few things Steve needs to keep himself happy. The first and foremost is to write, the second is to incite political activism through the use of spoken word, third, he sees himself in an academic environment. It is his commitment to words and the need to constantly expand his mind that defines him. And finally, he wants a record deal, so that he can distribute his progressive and revolutionary ideas to the masses. A far cry from the fried chicken rap of yesterday, I'd say.

# BLUE

**Steve Colman**

I'm sorry to hear
That you are feeling blue
But blue is not such a bad thing
It is the color of the sky
And so it is the color of the sea
Because blue is the color of reflection
Sometimes it is the color I turn
When I hold my breath
It is par of the name
of a jazz club in New York City
Blue is a mood
A note
The color of survival
Because blue is like black
Strong and resilient
Pounding a smile from a frown
Blue is the sound of whales
Composing symphonies near blue icebergs
Blue is the past tense of blow
Which means the future is now
Blue can be royal navy Deep
Can be the moon
Can be you
Can be blue

# OUR HEROES

Steve Colman

one of our heroes
beat the shit out
of two homeless men
on 38th street last night
one of our heroes
kicked their legs with
his thickkk black boots
still ashy white with the residue
of the dust from the world
   trade center
one of our heroes
cracked the bottoms of their
   feet
with his flashlight
probably the same flashlight
he used to search for
victims buried beneath the rub-
   ble
near Wall Street.
victims who left families
with late mortgage payments
and medical bills
innocent workers whose
children
sleep near sidewalks
now

searching for food between the
   american
flags and fake eagle busts on
   fifth avenue
waiting for the freedom
Paul McCartney promised
or praying for a piece
while the city receives disaster
   relief
by watching the Yankees bomb
One of our heroes demon-
   strated
how to ground zero into nothing
last night
the precision timing
of his blows pierced the steel
souls on their soiled work
   shoes
the simple mathematics
of pain inflicted on their toes
on a crowded street in midtown
never made the nightly news.

# ROOM and BORED
## (one of those bitter love poems)

**Steve Colman**

I fell in love with you
because I was bored
tired
of watching the seasons change
by myself

so don't think
these tears are for losing you

they are
for the passing of time
alone

*Suheir* HAMMAD

The title of one of Suheir Hammad's books, *Born Palestinian, Born Black* gives insight into not only how she grew up, but also into how she sees and identifies herself as a result. Suheir refers to herself as "a Palestinian of African descent."

In Sunset Park, Brooklyn, if you weren't white, you automatically became either Black or Puerto Rican. And although the neighborhood had a growing and vibrant Arab population, **young Suheir** identified with the few Black kids in the neighborhood. Her father was a politically active Palestinian national, so she was raised to be aware of the political inequities that face all "Third World" peoples. A skinny girl with bushy black hair and thick glasses, she was not very popular and spent much of her time with her head in some book or another—which helps to explain why she's one of the most accomplished poets on the scene today. But the fruits of her voracious intellectual labor were not always embraced by peers nor supported by teachers. She recalls one incident where a teacher doubted that she'd read Tolstoy's *Anna Karenina* and humiliated her publicly by demanding a verbal recounting of the novel's story line. When she finished, she wasn't even offered an apology. This and similar incidents further cemented her feeling aware of her "otherness."

suheir hammad

As with many little colored girls who look nothing like the flaxen images smiling back at them from TV and movie screens, billboards, and magazines, demanding to be worshiped as the only possible beauty, she considered herself ugly by comparison. Not until her teen years and the emergence of evidence of the influence adolescent hormones can exert on the female body did she begin to feel attractive. Considered to be another light-skinned, curly-haired, "yellow" girl, and therefore automatically "pretty" by Black teengaed boys, young Suheir did not have any trouble attracting attention from them.

As with many of the teens of the time, the growing Hip Hop culture was a draw. Working at a supermarket in Hollis, Queens (home of Run-DMC), she did graffiti and wrote rhymes, a precursor to the poetry to come. At times her newly assumed urban lifestyle put her at odds with her more traditional Islamic parents, but Suheir was not abandoning her Palestinian roots. Organically, the two lives she lived simultaneously as both Palestinian *and* Black melded, producing a unique political awareness that included both the culture she had been born to *and* the one she had so willingly immersed herself in.

Just as she had not forsaken the culture of her birth for another, neither had her love of hip-hop curbed her incessant need to read. As she read many of the leading revolutionary scholars of the 1960s, her interests naturally took on a more radical tone. Suheir was able to gather a broad understanding of the worldwide struggle against oppression, comprehending the Middle East situation within the context of other struggles happening around the globe. The feelings of "otherness" she felt as a child abated in direct proportion to the growth of her solidarity with her own people as well as with "others." In college, that solidarity fueled a burgeoning activism and radical politics—"radical" meaning "original," "fundamental," "basic," "innate."

Compelled to speak out, Suheir picked up the pen and wrote poetry, adding fodder to her own political fire. That pen explored deep wellsprings of personal feelings, bone-chilling historical "fact," and genocidal current events. Her work emerged as yet another blend that has so characterized Suheir's life, this one being of both an individual *and* a collective self-exploration.

It is within the confluence of all this that Suheir came to the Broadway stage, where she hoped her poems sparked a flame of social justice inside of someone else. So when asked if she minded reciting the same material every night, her answer is a resounding NO! She found her motivation in that yet-to-be-born radical, just out for an evening of entertainment.

Some would let all the media attention that she gets go to their head, but not Suheir. She says she doesn't feel like a "star" and that all the good things that are happening are "Divine Grace." Her aspirations are simple. She just wants to be better at what she does best: composing poetry and living her life. Every time she goes on stage, she asks God for continued Grace, Compassion, and Light. It seems that God has granted her that, along with the melodically harmonious ability to be both Palestinian *and* Black.

# on the
# BRINK OF...

**Suheir Hammad**

On the brink of
tears, sanity and war,
I feel powerless, hope
less and less than alive.

What do we tell young
people? How do we say, "...your
voice means nothing to those
who think life is about power
over others and greed?" And where
is it safe to think for yourself and try
real hard to not want to hurt nobody?

I don't want to hurt nobody, God knows.

In Iraq, children are looking towards
the night sky with fear, as though
there were no stars, only bombs in the cosmos.
And they are afraid of the earth because
they can count the cancers in their
hoods now, where once there were none. And
how do I tell American youth
that popular culture means nothing to
justice and everything to keeping them
numb to the world? And how do I
scream when I have no voice left? And who
will answer these questions for me?

Not Rachel Corrie. She is dead. And no matter
what any army says, I have seen the photos
and that woman was wearing orange,
bright and alive one minute and dying
under rubble the next. Even I, it seems, have
developed a callous to the deaths of
Palestinians, because the murder of this white
girl from Olympia Washington has
my heart breaking and my blood faint. Something
like ten Palestinians have been killed since
yesterday, when a Caterpillar bulldozer driven
by a man demolished the home that was her body.

If anyone knows her family, please relay
to them my grief and my sorry.

You can still find her phone number
on the Internet for meetings and organizing. You
can still read her accounts of being in Palestine.
She was a good writer. There are
people who are writing,

"She should not have been there in the first place"
Now she is dead.

"Good riddance"
Now she is dead.

"Treasonous bitch"
Now she is dead.

What do I tell young people about non
violence when they can see for themselves
how even orange bright and megaphone loud

and cameras and US citizenship will
not stop your murder? I recall
the days black boys were lynched and dis
membered for looking at white women, now
tax dollars are crushing dissent wherever it blooms.

Human shields for human targets.

There are words I am taking back. I reclaim them and will
no longer allow anyone to dictate my language. There is
no "right wing" a wing is of nature, and murder may be
    human, but
it is not natural, even if animals eat each other, is that
    what we
are then, animals? If so claim it, motherfucker.

There is no "mother of all bombs." Blair, Sharon, Bush, all
    have
mothers and no matter what they do, there is something
they love. White power, oil, the need to be God's only
chosen, whatever, but they love something, because their
    mothers
loved them. A bomb loves nothing, has no mother and is
    not about
life. There is no mother of all bombs,
only more mankind self-destruction.

There is no safety in being a bully. I know
because I have been bullied and I know now,
with my first grey hair and all, that authentic
power is not about others but about self.

This is not a poem. This is not a threat. This
is a promise. God has a better imagination
than all of us combined and I do not
know what form retribution will take, but
I have seen karma happen and it will
again, and when it does I will chant
the names of the innocent and I will stand
with those who have kept their hands clean of blood
and their hearts clear of hate.

It is hard not to hate right now. But I
have been loved, I have loved and I know
that those who de-humanize their enemy are
only doing so to themselves. Peace work
is justice work is God's work. Rachel Corrie wrote,

"Nevertheless, I think about the fact that no amount of
reading, attendance at conferences, documentary viewing
and word of mouth could have prepared me for the reality
of the situation here. You just can't imagine it unless you
see it, and even then you are always well aware that your
experience is not at all the reality: what with the
difficulties the Israeli Army would face if they shot an
unarmed U.S. citizen, and with the fact that I have money
to buy water when the army destroys wells, and, of
course, the fact that I have the option of leaving. Nobody
in my family has been shot, driving in their car, by a rocket
launcher from a tower at the end of a major street in my
hometown. I have a home. I am allowed to go see the
ocean."

She is dead now. And the ocean
will miss her gaze. Palestine will miss
her heart, but mostly her family will
miss her breath. And the president of the United States of
     America
(when did that happen again?) has all
but declared war on Iraq, and so more deaths are
     promised.

What do I tell young people about any
thing? Especially humanity and morality. Slightly
a month before her murder Rachel wrote home,

"Many people want their voices to be heard, and I think
we need to use some of our privilege as internationals to
get those voices heard directly in the U.S., rather than
through the filter of well meaning internationals such as
myself. I am just beginning to learn, from what I expect to
be a very intense tutelage, about the ability of people to
organize against all odds, and to resist against all odds."

More words I reclaim – Hero, Brave, Soldier. This
young woman did the un-thinkable, she did not
blink, did not half step, did not back
down in the face of death. What greater odds than
one lone female frame against a destructive machine?

What greater story to tell?

On the brink of war, may our power
come from the people Rachel Corrie was murdered
defending. On the brink of war, may our hope
come from one another. On the

brink of – wait – this is not a war.
on the brink of whatever new fangled
imperialist project this is, may Rachel Corrie
live in our resistance, in our pursuit
of justice, and in the spirit of sisterhood. On
the brink of war, may we remember how divine
human beings can be.

*"Rachel Corrie Will Live in Our Resistance" was a sign made and
carried by Suzan Hammad at Rachel Corrie's vigil in New York City.

*"The Power is With the People," said most recently by Sabrine
Hammad about her own remarkable activist work. Thank you to both
of my sisters, who are my heroes.

*For more information, and unbelievable photographs of Rachel
Corrie's murder, log onto: www.ElectronicIntifada.org

suheir hammad

# *the gift*
# of MEMORY

**Suheir Hammad**

Who will mutter
The mighty acts of israel
Muster declarations
Of shrapnel truth

The dead will they
Speak to silences swallowed
With bulldozed earth

The dead will they
Bear skeletal witness
To their own lives
Remind us long after
Headline ink

Up rise and search
Out behind rocks trees
Behind peace and paper
Search out god's ear
To whisper the truth
They know

The poets the
Doctors the
Emergency room politicians
Who will report
These acts

Of gods
Ordered by men

The dead will they recite
Recall rewind
The videotape
Of the dead
Forget will the living
Remember

To remind us we
Are reaping what was
Sown the dead fruit
Of mangled roots

# NOTHIN
## to waste

**Suheir Hammad**

you don't waste nothin you
know the worth of
bread cupcakes carrots gummi bears whatever
falls gets picked up and
kissed up to god

and it's new and
fresh again good
enough to eat to
place on the table

and what about cherries busted and
sweet meat flesh about
stretch of leg tear of
muscle what about
almond surprise jelly jam pumpkin virgin puddin

can she pick herself
up back to the table and
know her worth kiss
and make herself new
like chocolate frostin and yellow
rice good enough

pick herself up and
kiss herself there kiss
herself back kiss
herself back and
up to god

# the GIVERS

Suheir Hammad

this is modest beauty
a lowered gaze, muted color
a flutter, shadows
a murmur

i am looking for history
in neon lights, billboards
splayed on chests
but this is quiet
beauty

and i need to sit
still, concentrate to hear
the blood below my
feet, the spirits in
the wind, on me

under every stone a myth
behind every branch a prophesy

trees here bear fruit as
sisters bear life
as duty and beauty both
giving and rooted

trees here stand, roots
apart, branches on trunks
necks turned to go
and say, "girl, where
you been
what you
bring, drink some tea,
we got stories to tell you"

# DJ
## TENDAJI

# "DJ Tendaji on the Wheels of Steel. Please

give it up for the DJ!" Everyone's heard that command before, "Give it up for the DJ!" but not echoing off the hallowed walls of a Broadway stage.

It all began during his college years. Tendaji had friends who were DJs, so he began fooling around with the turntables as a hobby. To his surprise, he had a natural, **INTUITIVE TALENT** for selecting music to evoke any mood he wanted. That talent is very much evident in the way he moved the performances of *Def Poetry* from one scene to another on beats that effortlessly hinge the transitions. While that type of precision might be smooth to Tendaji, the progression from being a club DJ to being a performer on the stage was a little more challenging.

Tendaji is no stranger to stage sets. At an early age, he spent lots of time hanging with his dad, director Stan Lathan, on various TV and movie sets, the most memorable being the set of the famous hip-hop movie *Beat Street*. It left a lasting impression on him and fostered a desire to follow in his father's footsteps and become a director himself; a path he's already traveled, having served as assistant director on the *Steve Harvey Show* and various other T.V. shows and music videos. Although he had experience on the road with Cedric the Entertainer as his DJ, playing the same music, saying the same lines, hitting the same cues with

dj tendaji

the same fire as the first time, was challenging in the opening weeks of the play. As he settled in and allowed himself to feel the rhythm of the audiences, he says it's those connections that get him as deeply into one show as the next—there's always an old head or two that is ready to nod to Frankie Beverly and Maze.

*Def Poetry on Broadway* has been a great experience for him. But unlike the other performers in the play, he wants to get back behind the scenes, behind the camera. In addition to his TV experience, he's already produced one short film that won acclaim and is working on the finances to do a feature-length production. In the meantime, he's doing his DJ thing at some of the hipper downtown clubs in the Big Apple while he's here. Even though he's DJ'ed his way all the way to Broadway, he recognizes its limits as a profession. When the show closes, he's headed back to Los Angeles to pursue his dreams of making films.

# TENDAJI'S
## TOP TEN
# HIP-HOP JOINTS/
# R&B CLUB JOINTS
## (no particular order)

1) Jay-Z / "I Just Wanna Love You (Give It to Me)"

2) Tupac / "I Get Around"

3) Notorious B.I.G. / "One More Chance (remix)"

4) Snoop Dog / "Ain't No Fun"

5) Usher / "You Don't Have to Call"

6) Rakim / "I Ain't No Joke"

7) Ludacris / "Move Bitch"

8) Gang Starr feat. Nice & Smooth / "Dwyck"

9) Total / "Can't You See"

10) Method Man & Redman / "Da Rockwilder"

dj tendaji

# TOP TEN
## OLD SCHOOL
## CLUB JOINTS
### (no particular order)

1) Cheryl Lynn / "Encore"

2) Marvin Gaye / "Got to Give It Up"

3) Michael Jackson / "P.Y.T."

4) Maze feat. Frankie Beverly / "Before I Let Go"

5) Jones Girls / "Nights Over Egypt"

6) Guy / "I Like"

7) Prince / "If I Was Your Girlfriend"

8) Gil Scott-Heron / "The Bottle"

9) Chaka Khan / "Ain't Nobody"

10) Stevie Wonder / "All I Do"

def poetry jam on broadway

# AUTHOR INDEX

# FIRST LINE INDEX